A GUIDE

TO

COPIES & ABSTRACTS

OF

IRISH WILLS

EDITED BY THE

REV. WALLACE CLARE.

CLEARFIELD COMPANY
REPRINTS & REMAINDERS

Originally Published As
Irish Genealogical Guides, First Series
Volume One (All Published)
March, England
1930

Reprinted
Genealogical Publishing Co., Inc.
Baltimore, 1972

Reprinted for Clearfield Company Inc. by
Genealogical Publishing Co. Inc.
Baltimore, MD 1989

Library of Congress Catalogue Card Number 72-157438
International Standard Book Number 0-8063-0515-0

Made in the United States of America

PREFACE.

Wills being of paramount importance for the study of family and social history, the act of vandalism by which the buildings of the Four Courts, Dublin, were destroyed on the 30th June, 1922, has proved to be a serious set-back to genealogical research, as all the original wills deposited therein at the time, with the exception of only one Consistorial and eleven Prerogative wills, were burned; many other documents of national importance met a similar fate. Fortunately, however, prior to the disaster, genealogists had copied, from time to time, many thousands of these wills and the results of their labours had been ofttimes published in archæological and genealogical journals and family histories, or presented to libraries.

This, the First Volume of Irish Genealogical Guides, which is a small contribution towards the work of reconstructing testamentary records, contains; (a) A list of copies and abstracts of Irish wills deposited in the library of the Society of Genealogists, London, which I indexed in 1929, the excellent abstracts presented by W. H. Welply, Esq., of Belfast, forming the bulk of this fine collection. (b) A list which I made in 1929 at the Public Record Office, Dublin, of the copies of wills contained in all the Prerogative Will Books which were salved, namely, those for the years 1664-1684; 1706-1708, A—W; 1726-1728, A—W; 1728-1729, A—W; 1777, A—L; 1813, K—Z; 1834, A—E; (c) A list of a few early original wills deposited in England. (d) A list of copies and abstracts of wills contained in a few archæological and genealogical journals, family histories, etc.

Throughout this volume the ortographical rendering of surnames as given in the copies and abstracts of wills has been retained, thus every likely form must be consulted.

The following points should be kept in mind by all Irish Pedigree-hunters: 1. There are still in existence some original wills to be found in many a family deed-box up and down the country, for a number of the earlier documents of this nature never found their way to the Public Record Office, Dublin. 2. The MSS. at the Office of Arms, Dublin Castle, include abstracts from practically all the old Irish Prerogative Wills. 3. A fine collection of official copies of wills, original unproved wills and abstracts from testamentary records, is to be found at the Public Record Office, Dublin.The 55th Annual Report of the Deputy Keeper of the Public Records in Southern Ireland, published in 1928, is a reference book of the greatest value, being a mine of information concerning the Records which have been salved, etc. 4. A Public Record Office for Northern Ireland has been established at Belfast, and shows every sign of becoming a genuine treasure-house, and will fully repay a visit. The interesting Report of the Deputy Keeper of the Records of Northern Ireland (1928) contains reports on the Downshire Family Letters, 1790-1793; the Archdale Papers, 1537-1909; the Lennox-Conyngham Papers, 1630-1759; and the Verner and Ranfurly Papers 1671-1874. 5. The library of the Society of Genealogists, 5 Bloomsbury Square, London, W.C. 1., is open to non-members on payment of a fee of 5/- per day.

My sincere thanks are due to all subscribers: to the Deputy Keeper of the Public Records of Southern Ireland, who has permitted the publication of the Will Book indices; to Dr. C. Corker Vigurs, for allowing me to copy the abstracts from the Corker wills in his possession; to the Secretary of the Society of Genealogists, for her unfailing help, and to Messrs. R. F. Wayte and D. Forrester, for their invaluable assistance.

The Second Volume of this publication will appear in 1931 and will contain references to over four thousand Irish Wills.

The Presbytery,   WALLACE CLARE.

March, Cambridgeshire.

St. Patrick's Day, 1930.

Key to Reference Letters.

A. The Journal of the Royal Society of Antiquaries of Ireland, founded in 1849 as the Kilkenny Archæological Society.

B. Register of Wills and Inventories of the Diocese of Dublin, 1457-83, edited by Henry F. Berry, M.A. (Dublin 1898).

C. MS. Book of Abstracts from Wills by the Rev. W. Clare, Library of the Society of Genealogists, London.

D. Records relating to the Diocese of Ardagh and Clonmacnoise, by the Very Rev. John Canon Monahan (Dublin 1886).

E. The Diary of George Booth of Chester, by the Rev. G. Payne Crawford (Chester 1928).

F. The Family of Green of Youghal, by the Rev. H. Swanzy and T. Green (1902).

G. MS. Copies and Abstracts of Irish Wills by W. H. Welply, Esq., B.A., and others, Library of the Soc. of Genealogists, London (D.MSS. 345).

H. The Family History of Hart of Donegal, by H. Travers Hart. (1907).

J. Calendar of Carew MSS.

L. Some Notes on the Lowthers who held Judicial Office in Ireland in the 17th Century, by Sir E. Bewley, LL.D.

M. Journal of the Irish Memorials Association, formerly the Association for the Preservation of the Memorials of the Dead in Ireland.

N. Notes and Queries.

O. Wills deposited at Somerset House, London.

P. Copies of Wills filed under "Places (Ireland)," Soc. of Genealogists, London.

Q. A Quantock Family, by Col. G. Dodsworth Stawell. (1910).

R. Chester Archæological Society's Journal.

S. Copies of Wills filed under "Surnames," Library of Soc. of Genealogists, London.

T. Registrum Testamentorum Dioces, Dublin, Tempore Jo. Archiep., Trinity College Library, Dublin (MS. E. 3.32).

U. History of the Family of White, by John Davis White.

W. Will Books deposited at the Public Record Office, Dublin.

X. Wills deposited at the Probate Registry, Chester.

Y. Wills deposited at the Probate Registry, York.

Z. Irish Builder.

A GUIDE

TO

COPIES & ABSTRACTS

OF

IRISH WILLS.

FIRST SERIES.

Date of Probate.		REFERENCE
1834.	**Abbott,** Benjamin, Dublin.	W.
1777.	,, Joyce, spinster, Dublin.	W.
1717.	,, Thomas, Charleville, Co. Cork.	G.
1834.	**Acheson,** William, Derrynatowny, Co. Leitrim.	W.
1666.	**Adaire,** William, Ballymanagh, Co. Antrim.	W.
1729.	**Adams,** Robert, Heathstown, Co. Meath.	W.
1763.	**Adderley,** Dorothy, widow, Bandon, Co. Cork.	G.
1719.	,, Francis, Drumkeen, Co. Cork.	G.
1649.	,, Capt. Thomas, Ballyneboy, Co. Cork.	G.
1658.	,, Thomas, Innishannon, Co. Cork.	G.
1691.	,, Thomas, Innishannon, Co. Cork.	G.
1791.	,, Thomas, Innishannon, Co. Cork.	G.
1773	**Addis,** Fenton, Summerhill, Co. Cork.	G.
1665.	,, John, yeoman, Frompton, Glos.	W.
1742.	,, John, merchant, Cork.	G.
1834.	**Agnew,** Edward Jones, Kilwanghter Castle, Co. Antrim.	W.
1834.	**Aickin,** Samuel, attorney, Dublin.	W.
1727.	**Aigoin,** John, merchant, Dublin.	W.
1777.	,, Margaret, spinster, Dublin.	W.
1681.	**Aland,** Henry, Waterford.	W.
1683.	,, Henry, Waterford.	W.

NOTE.—An asterisk denotes the date of the will and not the year of probate.

IRISH WILLS: COPIES AND ABSTRACTS.

Date of
Probate.

REFERENCE.

1834.	**Alcock,** Beata, widow, formerly of Wexford, now of Dublin.	W.
1834.	,, Eliza Jane, spinster, Wexford.	W.
1834.	,, John, Kingstown Harbour, Co. Dublin.	W.
1727.	,, Simon, Dublin.	W.
1777.	,, Thomas, Waterford.	W.
1834.	**Aldwell,** Anne, widow, Mitchelestown, Co. Cork.	W.
1834.	**Alexander,** John Lynch, Galway.	W.
1726.	,, Richard James, Mawdlins, Co. Meath.	W.
1726.	**Allen,** John, Lord Viscount of the Kingdom of Ireland.	W.
1666.	,, Dame Mary, widow, Lutterelstown, Co. Dublin.	W.
1666.	,, Patrick, Dublin.	W.
1726.	,, Richard, Monaghan.	W.
1830.*	,, Richmond, Eccles Street, Dublin.	A.1876-8, p.333.
1728.	**Alley,** Mary, widow, Cork.	W. & G.
1693.	,, Thomas, Rathcormac, Co. Cork.	G.
1834.	**Alleyn,** Charles, Ballynacky, Co. Cork.	W.
1683.	**Alsop,** Grace, alias **Mee,** Upper Coomb, Co. Dublin.	W. & G.
1667.	**Amory,** Thomas, Galy, Co. Kerry.	W.
1728.	,, Thomas, Bunratty, Co. Clare.	W.
1729.	**Anderson,** Gregory, distiller, Dublin.	W.
1706.	,, James, Belfast.	W.
1834.	,, John, Dublin.	W.
1834.	,, Richard, soap-boiler, Sligo.	W.
1729.	,, Thomas, Cloncannon, King's Co.	W.
1668.	**Andrews,** William, Finglas, Co. Dublin.	W.
1737.	**Anglesey,** Arthur, Earl of.	G.
1711.	,, James, Earl of.	G.
1711.	,, John, Earl of.	G.
1759.*	,, Richard, Earl of.	G.
1777.	,, Juliana, Countess Dowager.	W. & G.
1726.	**Anster,** Martin, merchant, Charleville, Co. Cork.	W.
1726.	**Archbold,** Joan.	W.
1834.	,, Michael, farmer, Cookestown, Co. Kildare	W.
1726.	**Archbould,** Anthony, victualler, Dublin.	W.
1733.	**Archer,** Clement, Enniscorthy, Co. Wexford.	G.

IRISH WILLS: COPIES AND ABSTRACTS.

Date of Probate.			REFERENCE.
1763.	**Archer,** Elizabeth, widow, Dublin.		G.
1730.	,,	Henry, merchant, Enniscorthy, Co. Wexford.	G.
1834.	,,	Henry, Ballyseskin, Co. Wexford.	W.
1662.*	,,	James, gent., Freshford, Kilkenny.	A. 1867, p.230.
1602.*	,,	John, Fitz-Lawrence, burgess, Kilkenny.	A. 1867, p.229.
1574.*	,,	Lawrence, Kilkenny.	A. 1867, p.230.
1681.*	,,	Luke, priest, Kilkenny.	A. 1867, p.230.
1729.*	,,	Martin, Kilkenny.	A. 1867, p.230.
1722.*	,,	Martin, priest, Kilkenny.	A. 1867, p.230.
1605.*	,,	Megge Fitz-Edward, alias **Roth,** widow, Kilkenny.	A. 1867, p.229.
1536.*	,,	Peter, Kilkenny.	A. 1867, p.229.
1777.	,,	Richard, merchant, Cork.	W.
1733.	,,	Robert, Dublin.	G.
1617.*	,,	Thomas Fitz-Walter, alderman, Kilkenny.	A. 1867, p.229
1707.	**Armar,** Rev. William, archdn., of Connor, Ballybrittan, Co. Antrim.		W.
1834.	**Armstrong,** Francis, Dublin.		W.
1777.	,,	John, silkweaver, Dublin.	W.
1727.	,,	William, Endrene, King's Co.	W.
1834.	**Arnot,** Archibald, Bushtown, Londonderry.		W.
1666.	**Arthur,** John Dublin.		W.
1666.	,,	John Fitz-Robert, Dublin.	W.
1649.	,,	Robert, alderman, Dublin.	W.
1729.	,,	Thomas Fitz-Francis, Limerick.	W.
1717.	**Ashe,** St. George, Bishop of Derry.		G.
1834.	,,	Henry, Chelsea, London.	W.
1834.	,,	Rev. Isaac, Tanlaght Glebe, Co. Derry.	W.
1665.	,,	Nicholas, Moyrath, Co. Meath.	W.
1727.	,,	Richard, Ashefield, Co. Meath.	W. & G.
1722.*	,,	Thomas, St. John's, Co. Meath.	G.
1682.	,,	William, Ashefield, Co. Meath.	W.
1665.	**Ashenhurst,** Peter, Dublin.		W.
1671.	**Aston,** Sir William, Kt., Richardstown, Co. Louth.		G.
1708.	**Arkin,** John, alderman, Youghal, Co. Cork.		W.
1682.	**Atkins,** Augustus, Cork.		G.
1664.	**Atkinson,** Anthony, Camgort, King's Co.		W.

IRISH WILLS: COPIES AND ABSTRACTS.

Date of Probate.		REFERENCE.
1834.	**Atkinson,** Maria Elenor, alias **Ledwith,** widow, Newry.	W.
1777.	,, Sarah, spinster.	W.
1706.	**Aubin,** Elias, French refugee, City Cork.	W.
1726.	**Auchmuty,** or **Achmuty,** John, Newtown, Co. Longford.	W.
1727.	**Aughmuty,** Charles, merchant, Dublin.	W.
1768.	**Austen,** Joseph, Cork.	G.
1761.	**Austin,** Joseph, alderman, Cork.	G.
1728.	,, Richard, farmer, Corballis, Co. Meath.	W.
1683.	**Avery,** Samuel, alderman, London.	W.
1683.	**Awbrey,** William, Stephen St., Dublin.	W.
1834.	**Aylmer,** Arthur, lieut., Walworth Castle, Durham.	W.
1777.	**Aylward,** Sarah, widow, Dublin.	W.
1772.	**Bacon,** Benjamin, Glebe Hall, Co. Derry.	G.
1708.	,, Dorothy, widow, Rathkeny, Co. Tipperary.	W.
1709.	,, Edward, Doulin, Co. Londonderry.	G.
1776.	,, Mary, widow, Wyanstown, Co. Dublin.	G.
1610.*	,, Robert, Dublin.	G.
1746.	,, Robert, Tamlaghtfinlagan, Co. Derry.	G.
1705.	,, William, Tamlaghtard, Co. Derry.	G.
1781.*	**Baggs,** James, Lismore.	G.
1834.	**Bailey,** Thomas, shoemaker, Athy, Co. Kildare.	W.
1834.	**Bailie,** Robert Ellis, Shortstone, Co. Louth.	W.
1777.	**Baillie,** Andrew Thomas, merchant, Newry, Co. Down.	W.
1787.	,, James, Inishargie, Co. Down.	G.
1723.	**Baily,** Jane, widow.	G.
1666.	,, Penelope, widow, Gortman, Co. Cavan.	W.
1834.	**Baker,** Ann or Anna Maria, widow, Cork.	W.
1694.	,, Catherine, spinster, Shanagarry, Co. Cork.	G.
1683.	,, Edward, courier, Coombe, Dublin.	W.
1752.	,, John, vintner, Cork.	G.
1834.	**Bane,** Isaac, farmer, Drumon, Co. Armagh.	W.
1743.*	**Baldwin,** Henry, Garraneaghovny, Co. Cork.	G.
1696.	,, Herbert, Currinordy, Cork.	G.
1688.	,, James, Pollericke, Killmory, Cork.	G.
1769.	,, John, Bandon, Co. Cork.	G.

IRISH WILLS: COPIES AND ABSTRACTS.

Date of Probate.		REFERENCE.
1627.	**Baldwin,** Margery, widow, Templemartin, Co. Cork.	G.
1666.	,, Richard, Dublin.	W.
1768.	,, Walter, Roughgrove, Co. Cork.	G.
1727.	**Balfe,** Patrick, Cregg, Co. Meath.	W.
1721.	**Balfour,** Sir William, Westminster.	G.
1665.	**Ball,** John, merchant, Kilkenny.	W.
1666.	,, Richard, late Capt., Lieut. to Sir Thomas Armstrong.	W.
1777.	,, Stearne, clerk, Drogheda.	W.
1672.*	**Bankes,** Joseph, Dublin.	G.
1682.	,, Richard, Rector of Delgany, Co. Wicklow.	G.
1730.	,, Richard, clerk, Eyre Court, Co. Galway.	G.
1777.	**Banks,** Samuel, Atherdee, Co. Louth.	W.
1834.	**Barber,** Elizabeth, widow, Tullyquilly, Co. Down.	W.
1834.	**Babour,** John, The Plantation, Lisburn, Co. Antrim.	W.
1475.	**Barby,** John.	T. & B., p.154.
1708.	**Barker,** Francis, alderman, Waterford.	W.
1683.	,, George, vintner, Dublin.	W.
1727.	**Barlow,** Elizabeth, widow, Dublin.	W.
1726.	,, Lewis, Ballinaffiragh, Co. Westmeath.	W.
1746.	,, Ralph, Aghnamallagh, Co. Monaghan.	G.
1726.	,, William, Dublin.	W.
1683.	**Barnard,** William, Dublin.	W. & M., Vol. XI, p.511.
1834.	,, Rev. William Henry, Finmere, Oxford.	W.
1669.	**Barne,** Thomas, Erith, Kent.	W.
1681.	**Barnes,** Gabriel, merchant, Honiton, Devon.	W.
1707.	,, John, Dublin.	W
1726.	**Barnewall,** Elizabeth, spinster, Dublin.	W.
1710.	**Barnstable,** Charles, Castlebrett, Co. Cork.	G.
1834.	**Barr,** James, Coleraine, Co. Down.	W
1474.	**Barret,** Nicholas, St. Michan, Co. Dublin.	T. & B., p.70.
1729.	**Barrett,** Samuel, Castletown, Co. Catherlagh.	W.
1708.	**Barrington,** Alexander, Castletown.	G.
1778.	,, Alexander, Barretstown, Co. Kildare.	G.
1799.	,, Alexander, grocer, Coombe.	G.

IRISH WILLS: COPIES AND ABSTRACTS.

Date of Probate.			REFERENCE.
1733.	**Barrington,** Benjamin, Alderman, Limerick.		G.
1748.	,,	Benjamin, Dublin.	G.
1769.	,,	Benjamin, burgess, Limerick.	G.
1806.	,,	Benjamin Limerick.	G.
1749.	,,	Catherine, spinster.	G.
1687.	,,	Christopher, Logh Heoge, Queen's Co.	G.
1817.*	,,	Edward, Ballyhow, Co. Wexford.	G.
1758.	,,	Elizabeth, spinster, Dublin.	G.
1774.	,,	Elizabeth, spinster, Dublin.	G.
1753.*	,,	George, Ballinlusk.	G.
1762.*	,,	Jane, Barretstown, Co. Kildare.	G.
1784.	,,	John, tallow chandler, Dublin.	G.
1743.	,,	Joshua, Dublin.	G.
1753.	,,	Margaret, widow, Dublin.	G.
1796.	,,	Mary, widow, Hillbrook, Co. Dublin.	G.
1834.	,,	Mary, spinster, Dublin.	W.
1837.	,,	Nelson, Dublin.	G.
1668.	,,	Capt. Nicholas, Killone, Queen's Co.	G.
1747.	,,	Nicholas, Ballycogley, Co. Wexford.	G.
1770.	,,	Nicholas, Lambstown, Co. Wexford.	G.
1838.*	,,	Nicholas, Ballycogley, Co. Wexford.	G.
1746.	,,	Randolph, clerk.	G.
1784.	,,	Richard, farmer, Ballymacane, Co. Wexford.	G.
1758.	,,	Samuel, Ennis, Co. Clare.	G.
1749.	,,	Sarah, Dublin.	G.
1754.	,,	Wheeler, Dublin.	G.
1753.	,,	William, Raheenlush, Co. Wexford.	G.
1788.	,,	William, Queen's Co.	G.
1800.	,,	William, Ballyhegue, Co. Wexford.	G.
1808.	,,	William, Brittas.	G.
1834.	**Barron,** William, Monmahon, Co. Waterford.		W.
1729.	**Barry,** Elinor.		W.
1729.	,,	Elizabeth, widow, Dublin.	W.
1751.	,,	Elizabeth, widow, Dublin.	G.
1691.	,,	Garrett Oge, Ballymaeslyny, Co. Cork.	G

IRISH WILLS: COPIES AND ABSTRACTS.

Date of Probate.			Reference.
1751.	**Barry,** Henry, Lord Santry.		G.
1727.	,,	James, Dublin.	W.
1728.	,,	James, clerk, Dublin.	W.
1675.	,,	James, Sanbry.	G.
1727.	,,	James, Dublin.	G.
1834.	,,	Johanna, widow, Cork.	W.
1777.	,,	John, Ballyglissane, Co. Cork.	W.
1614.	,,	Redmond, James, Pollencurry.	G.
1690.	,,	Redmond, Rathcormick, Co. Cork.	G.
1739.	,,	Redmond, Ballyclogh, Co. Cork.	G.
1741.	,,	Redmond, Ballyclogh, Co. Cork.	G.
1750.	,,	Redmond, Rathcormick, Co. Cork.	G.
1779.	,,	Redmond, Cork.	G.
1790.	,,	Redmond.	G.
1639.	,,	Richard, Condonstown, Co. Cork.	G.
1661.	,,	Richard, Robertstown, Co. Cork.	G.
1699.	,,	Richard, Dublin.	G.
1777.	,,	Sprangor, King's Street, par. St. Paul, London.	W.
1727.	,,	Thomas, Dublin.	W.
1761.*	,,	Thomas, merchant, Cork.	G.
1757.	,,	William, Buttevant, Co. Cork.	G.
1710.	**Barter,** Francis, Templemichael, Co. Cork.		G.
1742.	,,	John, Cooldaniel, Co. Cork.	G.
1682.	,,	Thomas, Killeene, Co. Cork.	G.
1750.	,,	Thomas, Annaghmore, Co. Cork.	G.
1765.	,,	Thomas, Innishannon, Co. Cork.	G.
1769.	,,	Thomas, Innishannon, Co. Cork.	G.
1692.	,,	William, Templemichael, Co. Cork.	G.
1770.	,,	William, Affolard, Co. Cork.	G.
1728.	**Bastable,** Charles, Castlemagner, Co. Cork.		W.
1728.	**Bate,** Mary, widow, Kinsale, Co. Cork.		W.
1726.	**Bateman,** Susanna, widow, Coleraine, Co. Derry.		W.
1834.	**Bates,** Mary, alias **Kennedy,** widow, Naas, Co. Kildare.		W.
1666.	**Bathhurst,** Samuel, Dublin.		W.
1708.	**Batter,** Thomas, farmer, Aghaboe, King's Co.		W.

IRISH WILLS: COPIES AND ABSTRACTS.

Date of Probate.		REFERENCE
1834.	**Battesby,** Anna Maria, alias **Palmer,** widow, Dublin.	W.
1834.	**Baxter,** Robert, Glasslough, Co. Monaghan.	W.
1698.	**Bayly,** John, Castlemore, Co. Cork.	G.
1724.	,, John, Castlemore, Co. Cork.	G.
1777.	,, Thomas, Newtownbarry, Co. Wexford.	W.
1683.	**Beaghan,** Peter, Dublin.	W.
1834.	**Beale,** George Thomas, Cork.	W.
1729.	**Bean,** John, clothier, Dublin.	W.
1664.	**Bearde,** Thomas, Dublin.	W.
1701.	**Beare,** Richard, Moyalloe, Co. Cork.	G.
1719.	,, Richard, Mallow, Co. Cork.	G.
1834.	**Beasly,** Rebecca, spinster.	W.
1726.	**Beathom** (or **Beatham**), John, mariner, Dublin.	W.
1729.	**Beatty,** Claud, lieut., Coolerherty, Co. Longford.	W.
1681.	**Beatye,** John, Ferinsire, Killishandra, Co. Cavan.	W.
1777.	**Beaumont,** Thomasin, widow.	W.
1617.	**Becher,** Edward, Crookhaven, Co. Cork.	G.
1721.	,, Elizabeth, Aghadown, Co. Cork.	G.
1742.*	,, John, merchant, Bristol.	G.
1772.	,, Lionel, Sherkin Co., Cork.	G.
1726.	,, Michael, Aghadown, Co. Cork.	G.
1726.	,, Phane, Quarter-master-genl. of Lord Lieut.'s forces, Cork.	G.
1683.	**Bedel,** Ambrose, Carne, Co. Cavan.	W.
1726.	**Beecher,** Michael, Aghadown, Co. Cork.	W.
1834.	**Beere,** Martha, Leixlip, Co. Kildare.	W.
1612.	**Belcher,** Robert, carpenter, Shandon, Cork.	G.
1694.	,, Thomas, St. Finbarry's, Cork.	G.
1834.	**Bell,** David Beatson, Crail, Co. Fife.	W.
1834.	,, Margaret, spinster, Dublin.	W.
1729.	**Bellew,** Patrick, Thomastown, Co. Louth.	W.
1728.	**Bellings,** Garrett, linen-draper, Dublin .	W.
1473.	**Bellyng,** William, Belinstown.	T. & B., p.63.
1471.	**Bennet,** Alice, Santry.	T. & B., p.12.
1666.	**Bennett,** Ellen, widow, Dublin.	W.
1695.	,, Jane, widow, Cork.	G.

IRISH WILLS: COPIES AND ABSTRACTS.

Date of Probate.		REFERENCE.
1729.	**Bennett,** Robert, merchant, Dublin.	W.
1834.	**Bentley,** William, Hurlstown, Co. Clare.	W.
1666.	**Beresford,** Tristram, the elder, Coleraine, Londonderry.	W.
1834.	**Bergin,** Thomas, Ballina, Co. Mayo.	W.
1728.	**Berkley,** Dorothea, widow, Glasnevin, Co. Dublin.	W.
1707.	,, Rowland, Killeniffe, Co. Tipperary.	W.
1690.	**Bernard,** Francis, Castlemagher, Co. Cork.	G.
1731.*	,, Francis, Justice of Common Pleas, Dublin.	G.
1834.	,, Rebecca Margaretta, widow, Frankford, King's Co.	W.
1834.	,, Thomas, Castle Bernard, King's Co.	W.
1726.	**Berniere,** John Anthony, Lisburn, Co. Antrim.	W.
1834.	**Berrill,** Rose, widow, Drogheda.	W.
1834.	**Berry,** James Armstrong, Irishtown, Queen's Co.	W.
1728.	,, Robert, Dublin.	W.
1473.	,, Thomasin.	T. & B., p.61.
1729.	**Bessick,** Oliver, Dublin.	W.
1834.	**Best,** Rebecca, spinster, Caulfield, Dublin.	W.
1729.	,, Robert, Knockbeg, Queen's Co.	W.
1707.	**Bettesworth,** Peter, Ballydulea, Co. Cork.	W.
1729.	**Bevan,** Thomas, jun., Camas, Co. Limerick.	W.
1834.	**Bewley,** Mungo, Mountmellick, Queen's Co.	W.
1834.	**Bibby,** Richard, Kilkenny.	W.
1756.	**Biggs,** Edith, widow, Bandon, Co. Cork.	G.
1770.	,, Isaac, Bandon, Co. Cork.	G.
1772.	,, Jeremiah, clothier, Bandon, Co. Cork.	G.
1772.	,, Joseph, clothier, Bandon, Co. Cork.	G.
1775.	,, Rebecca, Bandon, Co. Cork.	G.
1726.	**Bignal,** Robert, merchant, Edenderry, King's Co.	W.
1664.	**Bigoe,** Philip, Newtown, King's Co.	W.
1665.	**Billingsley,** Elizabeth, alias **Worthell,** alias **Howell,** Ringsend.	W.
1728.	**Bindley,** Anne, widow, Dublin.	W.
1664.	**Bindon,** Henry, alderman.	W.
1834.	**Bingham,** Rev. Denis John Charles, Ballycastle, Co. Mayo.	W.
1728.	,, Lettice, widow of Sir Henry Bingham.	W.
1706.	**Birch,** Augustine, Ringsend, nr. Dublin.	W.

IRISH WILLS: COPIES AND ABSTRACTS.

Date of Probate.		REFERENCE.
1728.	**Bird,** Margaret, widow, Dublin.	W.
1683.	,, Oliver, merchant, Drogheda.	W.
1834.	**Birkett,** Henry, Carlow.	W.
1711.	**Bishop,** ———, widow.	G.
1834.	**Bishopp,** Very Rev. Sir Geo., Bt., Dean of Lismore.	W.
1834.	**Bissett,** Catherine, widow, Birr, King's Co.	W.
1728.	**Blackford,** William, Lisnover, Co. Cavan.	W.
1834.	**Blackmore,** Charles, Clonmel, Co. Tipperary.	W.
1777.	**Blake,** John, Balligloonine.	W.
1834.	**Bland,** Dorcas Letitia, spinster, Belfast.	W.
1728.	,, John, Blandsfort, Queen's Co.	W.
1726.	**Blany,** Baroness Margaret Dering, relict of Charles Dering.	W.
1834.	**Blayney,** Thomas Andrew, Lord of Castle Blayney, Co. Monaghan.	W.
1834.	**Bleakley,** Hannah, spinster, Downpatrick, Co. Down.	W.
1748.*	**Blennerhassett,** John, Tralee, Co. Kerry.	G.
1747.	,, Thomas, Tralee, Co. Kerry.	G.
1667.	**Bligh,** John, Rathmore, Co. Meath.	W.
1727.	**Blood,** William, merchant, Dublin.	W.
1834.	**Blosset,** John, Rathgar, Co. Dublin.	W.
1728.	**Blumfield,** Mary, St. Andrew's par., Dublin.	W.
1707.	**Blundell,** Sir. Francis, Bt., Edenderry, King's Co.	W.
1683.	,, Winwood, Ballinrath, King's Co.	W.
1727.	**Blyke,** Dudley, Kilcurley, Co. Louth.	W. & G.
1834.	**Bodkin,** Thomas Burke, Mount Silk, Co. Galway.	W.
1749.	**Bohilly,** Tige, Blarney Lane, Cork.	G.
1674.	**Boles,** Francis, Ballinlawbegg, Co. Cork.	G.
1788.	,, Francis, refiner, Moyge, Co. Cork.	G.
1739.*	,, John, Carrignashinny, Co. Cork.	G.
1704.	,, Jonathan, Killabrahir, Co. Cork.	G.
1834.	**Bolland,** Samuel, farmer, Farthingstown, Co. Westmeath.	W.
1781.	**Bonbonous,** John, clothier, Cork.	G.
1744.	,, Joseph, merchant, Cork.	G.
1714.	**Bond,** Christian, widow, Wexford.	G.
1834.	,, Hannah, widow, Rathcormac, Co. Cork.	W.
1688.	,, John, merchant, Wexford.	G.

IRISH WILLS: COPIES AND ABSTRACTS.

Date of Probate.   REFERENCE.

Date	Name	Reference
1726.	**Bonyng,** John, Cabraugh Lane, nr. Dublin.	W.
1670.	**Bor,** Begnett, alias **Cusack,** widow, Dublin.	G.
1637.	,, Christian, merchant, Dublin.	G.
1782.	,, Edward, Park, Co. Meath.	G.
1767.	,, Helena Maria, widow, Hammersmith.	G.
1723.	,, Jacob, Brigadier-General.	G.
1765.	,, Jacob, Dublin.	G.
1683.	,, John, merchant, Dublin.	W. & G.
1741.	,, John Dublin.	G.
1694.	,, Margaret, widow, Dublin.	G.
1686.	**Borr,** Christian, Drynagh, Wexford.	G.
1733.	,, Christian, Dublin.	G.
1477.	**Borrard,** John, Backweston.	T. & B., p.141.
1683.	**Boteler,** William, goldsmith, London.	W.
1707.	**Bourden,** Thomas, Suttonstrath, Co. Kilkenny.	W.
1472.	**Bourke,** Agnes, Balscaddan.	T. & B., p.46.
1728.	,, Joan, widow, Kilkenny.	W.
1667.	,, Sir John, Derrym'Loghery, Co. Limerick.	W.
1777.	,, Julian, widow, Brookhill, Co. Mayo.	W.
1834.	,, Richard, Court, Co. Wicklow.	W.
1726.	,, Theobald, Palmerstown, Co. Kildare.	W.
1667.	,, Thomas, Dublin.	W.
1777.	,, Ulick, Dublin.	W.
1727.	,, Walter, joiner, Dublin.	W.
1666.	,, William, Dublin.	W.
1726.	**Bourn,** Hugh, Dublin.	W.
1726.	**Bowen,** George, Derrinroe, Queen's Co.	W.
1729.	,, Nichol, Bowensford, Co. Cork.	W.
1764.*	**Bowerman,** Alice.	G.
1700.	,, Henry, Cooline, Co. Cork.	G.
1727.	**Bowyer,** Michael, Crannary, Co. Longford.	W.
1834.	**Boyd,** Alexander, Gortlee, Co. Donegal.	W.
1728.	**Boydell,** William, innkeeper, Kells, Co. Meath.	W.
1834.	**Boyle,** Hugh, Dungiven, Co. Derry.	W.
1471.	**Boys,** Richard, merchant, Coventry and Dublin.	T. & B., p.8.

IRISH WILLS: COPIES AND ABSTRACTS.

Date of Probate.		REFERENCE.
1729.	**Brabazon,** James, Carrstown.	W.
1772.*	**Braddell,** George, Bullingate, Co. Wicklow.	G.
1834.	,, Mary, spinster, Conyham, Co. Wicklow.	W.
1782.	,, William, woollen draper, Dublin.	G.
1726.	**Bradford,** Alex., Athy, Co. Kildare.	W.
1728.	**Bradish,** Wheaton, Kilkenny.	W.
1681.	**Bradshaw,** John, tanner, Lissebuck, Co. Monaghan.	W.
1834.	**Brady,** Amelia, spinster, Dublin.	W.
1777.	,, James, Carrigallen, Co. Leitrim.	W.
1777.	,, James, farmer, Kilpatrick.	W.
1834.	,, Nicholas, chandler, Dublin.	W.
1777.	,, Richard, Dublin.	W.
1728.	**Braithwait,** Samuel, clothier, Pimlico, Dublin.	W.
1834.	**Brandon,** Robert K. Drumadrachy, Co. Fermanagh.	W.
1707.	**Braughall,** Richard, merchant, Dublin.	W.
1599.	**Brayman,** John, Nurye, Ireland.	Y.Reg. Test. XXVII. 629.
1729.	**Bready,** John, yeoman, St. Thomas St., Dublin.	W.
1729.	**Bredin,** Catherine, widow.	W.
1728.	**Brereton,** Katherine, widow, Dublin.	W.
1834.	,, Mary, widow, Kildare.	W.
1718.	**Breton,** John, Cork.	G.
1688.	**Brettridge,** Roger, Castlebrettridge, Co. Cork.	W.
1834.	**Breviter,** Harriet, widow, Cork.	W.
1834.	**Brice,** Eliza, Whiteabbey, Co. Antrim.	W.
1707.	,, Penelope, widow, Dublin.	W.
1735.	**Bridgeman,** Elizabeth, Limerick.	G.
1728.	,, Henry, Woodfield, Co. Clare.	G.
1834.	**Bridges,** Catherine.	W.
1834.	,, Rev. Nathaniel, D.D., Clifton, England.	W.
1681.	,, Capt. Thomas, Somerset, Co. Londonderry.	W.
1777.	**Brierly,** Edward, Roscrea, Co. Tipperary.	W.
1664.	**Brinsmead,** Samuel, apothecary, Dublin.	W.
1834.	**Briscoe,** Henry, Tirvane House, Co. Tipperary.	W.
1834.	**Brison,** James, Killycor, Co. Derry.	W.

IRISH WILLS: COPIES AND ABSTRACTS.

Date of Probate.		REFERENCE.
1726.	**Britton,** John, Dublin.	W.
1707.	**Broadripp,** Samuel.	W.
1829.*	**Broadway,** Mary, Cove, Co. Cork.	C.
1712.	**Broderick,** Sir St. John, Kt., Ballyanon, Co. Cork.	G.
1728.	,, St. John, Midleton, Co. Cork.	W.
1707.	**Brogdon,** Elizabeth, alias **Jackson,** widow, Dublin.	W.
1768.	**Brome,** Rev. Samuel, Cork.	G.
1834.	**Brooke,** Sir Henry, Bart., Coolebrooke, Co. Fermanagh.	W.
1686.	**Brookeing,** Richard, Dublin.	G.
1681.	**Brookes,** Ann, widow, Limerick.	W.
1685.	**Brooking,** Joshua, Clonekilty, Co. Cork.	G.
1779.	**Broom,** George.	G.
1711.	**Broome,** Joshua, merchant tailor, Cork.	G
1834.	**Brophy,** Bartholomew, Castlecomer, Co. Kilkenny.	W.
1777.	**Broughton,** Mary, relict of Robt. Broughton.	W.
1777.	,, Mary, widow, Peter St., Dublin.	W.
1777.	,, Robert, Galway.	W.
1777.	**Brown,** Dominick, Castle Margaret, Co. Mayo.	W.
1777.	,, Dominick, Breafy, Co. Mayo.	W.
1777.	,, Francis, merchant, Dublin.	W.
1669.	,, John, merchant, Bandonbridge, Co. Cork.	G.
1834.	,, John, Bridgetown, Co. Clare.	W.
1743.	,, Thomas, Carlow.	G.
1777.	,, Thomas, Midleton, Co. Cork.	W.
1777.	,, Thomas, Co. Monaghan.	G.
1834.	,, Thomas, M.D., Mountpelier Hill, Dublin.	W.
1726.	,, Ulick, Fithmore, Co. Tipperary.	W.
1834.	**Browne,** Hon. Ann, widow, Dublin.	W.
1834.	,, Charles, Galway.	W.
1728.	,, Hannah Maria, widow, Dublin.	W.
1482.	,, John, Clondalkin.	T. & B., p.163.
1665.	,, John Dublin.	W.
1727.	,, John, Mullingar, Co. Westmeath.	W.
1729.	,, John, Ballynagallaugh, Co. Limerick.	W.
1729.	,, Julia, alias **Bellew,** widow, Dublin.	W.

IRISH WILLS; COPIES AND ABSTRACTS.

Date of Probate.		REFERENCE.
1884.	**Browne,** Mary, widow, Drogheda.	W.
1667.	,, Richard, Dublin.	W.
1884.	,, Richard Jebb, Newry, Co. Down.	W.
1729.	,, Thomas, alderman, Cork.	W.
1681.	,, Tobias, Currahine, Co. Cork.	W.
1467.	**Browneusyn,** Margaret, alias **Borrarde,** Killadoon.	T. & B., p.5.
1808.*	**Browning,** Hull, Dublin.	C.
1711.	**Brownlow,** Arthur, alias **Chamberlain,** Brownlowsderry, Co. Armagh.	G.
1808.	,, Catherine, widow, Dublin.	G.
1728.	,, James, Arbor Hill, Dublin.	W.
1721.	,, Jane, widow, Lurgan, Co. Armagh.	G.
1708.	,, William, Ballywilly, Co. Armagh.	G.
1789.	,, William Brownlowsderry, Co. Armagh.	G.
1716.	**Brownlowe,** John, alias **Chamberlaine,** Nisleiath, Co. Louth.	G.
1716.	,, Standish.	G.
1660.	,, Sir William, Kt., Brownlowsderry, Co. Armagh.	G.
1884.	**Brownrigg,** Anne, widow, Sandymount, Co. Dublin.	W.
1884.	,, Mary Jane, spinster, Wexford.	W.
1706.	**Brunton,** Anne, widow, Thomas' Court, Dublin.	G.
1690.	,, Anthony, Thomas, Court, Dublin.	G.
1707.	,, William, yeoman, Cabragh, Co. Dublin.	G.
1777.	**Bryan,** Pierse, Jenkinstown, Co. Kilkenny.	W.
1751.	**Bryen,** William, Mitchelstown, Co. Cork.	G.
1884.	**Bryne,** John, fisherman, Kingstown, Co. Dublin.	W.
1884.	**Buchanan,** John, Drummany, Co. Fermanagh.	W.
1884.	,, William, Ednasope, Co. Tyrone.	W.
1679.	**Buckeley,** Thomas, Dunkilt.	G.
1884.	**Buckley,** Elizabeth, widow, Dublin.	W.
1884.	,, John, shopkeeper, Millstreet, Co. Cork.	W.
1877.*	,, John, Kanturk, Co. Cork.	C.
1664.	**Buckworth,** Anthonie, Louth, rector of Killencoole.	W.
1702.	**Bulkeley,** Rev. John, Mallow, Co. Cork.	G.
1720.	,, Thomas, Kilkenny.	G.
1884.	**Bull,** Elizabeth, spinster, Northcourt, Isle of Wight.	W.

IRISH WILLS: COPIES AND ABSTRACTS.

Date of Probate.		REFERENCE.
1738.	**Bull,** Nathaniel, Grenanstown, Co. Meath.	G.
1729.	**Bullingbrook,** Rev. John, Castlreagh, Co. Roscommon.	W.
1726.	**Bullock,** John, timber-merchant, Dublin.	W.
1406.	**Bultingfort,** Richard, Limerick.	A. 1898, p.121.
1834.	**Bunbury,** Katherine, widow, Bath.	W.
1834.	**Bunn,** Benjamin, Dublin.	W.
1727.	**Bunworth,** Richard, Newmarket, Co. Cork.	W.
1834.	**Burden,** Mary, spinster, Ballmacarret, Co. Down.	W.
1834.	**Burdett,** George, Longtown House, Co. Kildare.	W.
1726.	,, Rev. John, Dean of Clonfert.	W.
1727.	,, Sir Thomas ,Bart., Garryhill, Co. Catherlogh.	W.
1718.	**Burges,** Thomas, Labacally, Co. Cork.	G.
1834.	**Burke,** Michael, Lakeview, Roscommon.	W.
1834.	,, William, Corylea, Co. Galway.	W.
1834.	**Burne,** Harriet, spinster, Kingstown, Co. Dublin.	W.
1707.	**Burnet,** James, saddler, Dublin.	W.
1834.	**Burns,** Elizabeth, Anne, Screebogue, Co. Longford.	W.
1708.	**Burridge,** Ezekiel, clerk, Dublin.	W.
1834.	**Burrowes,** Alexander Saunderson, Ballynicknakilly, Co. Down.	W.
1834.	,, Alexander, Carrowcrin, Co. Sligo.	W.
1834.	,, Alexander, Ferensboro', Co. Longford.	W.
1725.	,, Ann, widow, Butlerstown.	G.
1834.	,, Henry, apothecary, Dublin.	W.
1718.	,, James, merchant, Kinsale, Co. Cork.	G.
1688.	,, Thomas, Kinsale, Co. Cork.	G.
1777.	,, Thomas, cordwainer, Limerick.	W.
1834.	,, Sir Walter Dixon, Portarlington, Queen's Co.	W.
1689.	**Burt,** John, tailor, Dublin.	G.
1728.	**Burton,** Benjamin, alderman, Dublin.	W.
1728.	,, John, Borris-in-Ossory, Queen's Co.	W.
1834.	,, Rachel, spinster, Dublin.	W.
1834.	,, Dame Susan, alias **Meredyth,** widow, Pollerton, Co. Carlow.	W.
1666.	,, Thomas, Lismaranagan, Co. Cavan.	W.
1668.	,, Thomas, Estwicke, Shropshire.	W.
1767.*	,, Thomas, Dublin.	G.

IRISH WILLS: COPIES AND ABSTRACTS.

Date of Probate.		REFERENCE.
1834.	**Bury,** Alicia, widow, Downings, Co. Kildare, now of Dublin.	W.
1774.	**Bussy,** Mary, chandler, widow, Cork.	G.
1796.	**Busteed,** Jane, widow, Bandon, Co. Cork.	G.
1782.	,, Jonathan, Dundanion, Co. Cork.	G.
1760.	,, Michael, Killingley, Co. Cork.	G.
1712.*	,, Thomas, smith.	G.
1780.	,, Thomas, Ballinrea, Co. Cork.	G.
1817.	,, Thomas, Ballinrea, Co. Cork.	G.
1798.	,, William, Cork.	G.
1777.	**Butler,** Charles, mate of ship "Polly," Philadelphia.	W.
1707.	,, Edmond, Kinsale, Co. Cork.	W.
1777.	,, Rev. James, P.P., parish priest of Thurles.	W.
1834.	,, Hon. and Rev. James, Drumlease, Co. Leitrim.	W.
1727.	,, Peter, mariner, Waterford.	W.
1681.	,, Samuel, merchant, Dublin.	W.
1683.	**Butterton,** Jonathan, pewterer, Dublin.	W.
1834.	**Byrne,** Barnaby Joseph, Dublin.	W.
1729.	,, Bridget, widow, Wicklow, Co. Wicklow.	W.
1834.	,, Catherine, spinster, Dublin.	W.
1728.	,, Charles, Clone, Co. Wicklow.	W.
1777.	,, Elizabeth, widow of Dudley Byrne, grocer, Dublin.	W.
1777.	,, Elizabeth, spinster, Dublin.	W.
1834.	,, Mary, widow.	W.
1834.	,, Richard, farmer, Graigue, Queen's Co.	W.
1729.	,, Thomas, Wicklow, Co. Wicklow.	W.
1728.	**Cabanel,** Nathaniel.	W.
1665.	**Cadogan,** Elizabeth, widow, Ardraccan, Co. Meath.	W.
1834.	**Cahill,** Edmond, late of Castlewood, Queen's Co., now of Dublin.	W.
1777.	,, Hugh, merchant, Dublin.	W.
1834.	,, John, Ballymurphy, Co. Clare.	W.
1834.	**Calnen,** Joseph, goldsmith, Dublin.	W.
1727.	**Cairnes,** John, Dublin.	W.
1706.	,, William, Dublin.	W.
1834.	**Calcutt,** Dora Catherine, widow, Wilpark, Co. Galway.	W.
1707.	**Caldwell,** Christopher, Ballyhubbock, Co. Wicklow.	W.

IRISH WILLS: COPIES AND ABSTRACTS.

Date of Probate.   REFERENCE.

Date	Entry	Ref.
1834.	**Caldwell**, George, Dublin.	W.
1726.	,, Sir Henry, Bart, Castle Caldwell, Co. Fermenagh.	W.
1729.	,, Rev. William, Delgany, Co. Wicklow.	W.
1834.	**Calhoun**, John, barrister, Dublin.	W.
1777.	**Callaghan**, Christopher, farmer, Corduff, Co. Dublin.	W.
1834.	,, Richard, shopkeeper, Naas, Co. Kildare.	W.
1727.	,, Robert, Clonmeen, Co. Cork.	W.
1834.	**Callanan**, James Joseph, Cove, Co. Cork.	W.
1698.	**Calvert**, Thomas, Wexford.	G.
1726.	**Camack**, or **Camak**, John, farmer, Park Row, Co. Down.	W.
1729.	**Campbell**, Anne, spinster, Dublin.	W.
1834.	,, Denis, Dublin.	W.
1729.	,, John, Dublin.	W.
1757.	**Campion**, Jane, spinster, Cork.	G.
1796.	,, Martha, Cork.	G.
1700.	,, Thomas, Cork, late of Leitrim.	G.
1747.	,, Thomas, Cork.	G.
1761.	,, Thomas, Cork.	G.
1834.	**Cantley**, Catherine, widow, Stratford-St.-Mary, Suffolk.	W.
1834.	,, Thomas, clerk, Stratford-St.-Mary, Suffolk.	W.
1834.	**Card**, Rebecca, spinster, Bigoe, Co. Dublin.	W.
1721.	**Carew**, Robert, Ballinamona, Co. Waterford.	G.
1834.	**Carey**, Francis, Rush, Co. Dublin.	W.
1737.	,, Peter, Careysville, Co. Cork.	G.
1834.	**Carleton**, Catherine, Duxford, Cambs.	W.
1714.	**Carlton**, Isabelle, widow, Walshtown, Co. Cork.	G.
1834.	**Carncross**, John, Dublin.	W.
1834.	**Carolan**, Edward McDonnell, Carrickmacross, Co. Monaghan.	W.
1666.	**Caron**, Redmond, Dublin.	W.
1728.	**Carpenter**, John, Killanean, Co. Carlow.	W.
1834.	**Carr**, Rev. Thomas, priest, Dublin.	W.
1666.	**Carrick**, Anne, widow, Youghal, Co. Cork.	W.
1683.	**Carrol**, John, Garrans, King's Co.	W.
1728.	,, Nicholas, Stalleen, Co. Meath.	W.
1834.	**Carroll**, Elizabeth, spinster, Dublin.	W.

IRISH WILLS: COPIES AND ABSTRACTS.

Date of Probate.		REFERENCE.
1728.	**Carroll,** James, Tulla, Co. Tipperary.	W.
1834.	,, Mary Anne, Castlecomer, Co. Kilkenny.	W.
1834.	,, Robert Franklin, Limerick.	W.
1476.	**Carryk,** Dermot.	T. & B., p.139.
1475.	**Carryk,** William, Newcastle, nr. Lyons.	T. & B., p.106.
1834.	**Carson,** Elizabeth, widow, Bristol.	W.
1728.	,, Richard, yeoman, New Street, Dublin.	W.
1834.	**Carss,** Robert, Bury St. Edmunds, Suffolk.	W.
1834.	**Cartan,** Thomas, Coles Hall, Co. Wexford.	W.
1834.	**Carter,** Anne, spinster, Dublin.	W.
1834.	**Carty,** Thomas, farmer, Scourlogstown, Co. Westmeath.	W.
1757.	**Cary,** Henry Dungiven, Co. Derry.	N. v. 149, p.385.
1751.	,, Mordecai, Bishop of Killala.	M. v. XII, 369.
1777.	,, Rev. Oliver, Munfin, Co. Wexford.	W.
1726.	,, Tristram, Raphoe, Co. Donegal.	W.
1834.	**Casemy,** Robert, farmer, Sheepland, Co. Down.	W.
1763.	**Casey,** Elizabeth, Cork.	G.
1747.	,, John, starchman, Cork.	G.
1778.	,, John, Glanworth, Co. Cork.	G.
1834.	,, Matthew, Dublin, formerly of Roebuck, Co. Dublin.	W.
1834.	,, Patrick, Rosscarbery, Co. Cork.	W.
1769.	**Casey,** Thomas, farmer, Booleybeg, Co. Cork.	G.
1834.	**Cash,** Daniel, farmer, Ballinaclough, Co. Tipperary.	W.
1729.	**Cashel,** Timothy Goodwin, Archbishop of.	W.
1726.	,, William Palliser, Archbishop of.	W.
1727.	,, William Nicholson, Archbishop of	W.
1472.	**Cassell,** Alice, alias **Calff,** Lusk.	T. & B., p.58.
1834.	**Cassidy,** John, Monasterevan, Co. Kildare.	W.
1728.	**Castel,** Alexander, Ballyhack, Co. Wexford.	W.
1666.	**Castell,** Michael, merchant, London.	W.
1735.	**Catchcart,** Anne, widow, Belcoo, Co. Fermanagh.	G.
1665.	**Cathcart,** Adam, Drumslagee, Co. Tyrone.	W.
1720.	,, Allan, Enniskilling, Co. Fermanagh.	G.
1834.	**Caulfield,** Anna Maria, spinster, Booterstown, Co. Dublin.	W.
1834.	,, James, Castlestewart, Co. Tyrone.	W.

IRISH WILLS: COPIES AND ABSTRACTS.

Date of Probate.			REFERENCE.
1673.	**Causabon,** Thomas, Youghal, Co. Cork.		G.
1777.	**Cavanagh,** Jane, widow, Dunbrow, Co. Dublin.		W.
1707.	,, Murtagh, maltster, Dublin.		W.
1834.	,, Peter, Rathmines, Co. Dublin.		W.
1777.	,, or **Cavenagh,** Thomas, merchant, Dublin.		W.
1664.	**Cavenagh,** Edward, Dublin.		W.
1777.	**Cavendish,** Sir Henry, Bart., Doveridge, Derbyshire.		W.
1707.	**Chabenor,** Henry, Giltown, Co. Kildare.		W.
1834.	**Chadwick,** William, Willmount, Co. Tipperary.		W.
1726.	**Chalke,** Isaac, painter, Dublin.		W.
1613.	**Challoner,** Luke, D.D.		M. v. XI, p.368.
1681.	**Chalmers,** James, merchant, Belfast.		W.
1681.	**Chamberlain,** Walter, Dublin.		W.
1701.	**Chamberlaine,** John, Coomb.		G.
1625.*	,, Roger, Mizlegrath, Co. Louth.		G.
1686.	**Chamberline,** Peter, Killinetower, Co. Westmeath.		G.
1664.	**Chambers,** Edward, merchant, Dublin.		W.
1834.	,, James, architect, Blennerville, Co. Kerry.		W.
1597.	,, John, Dublin.		Y. Reg. Test. XVII. 37.
1768.	,, Susanna, alias **Barrington,** Mangin, Co. Wexford.		G.
1664.	,, Thomas, Armagh.		W.
1670.	**Chambre,** John, Stormonstown, Co. Louth.		G.
1687.	**Champion,** Jane, Cork.		G.
1689.	,, Thamzin, widow, Cork.		G.
1668.	,, William, felt-maker, Cork.		G.
1834.	**Chancellor,** John, watch-maker, Dublin.		W.
1727.	**Chandlee,** John, yeoman, Roosk, Kings Co.		W.
1707.	**Chapel,** Richard, Armagh.		W.
1792.	**Chapman,** Ann, widow, Dublin.		G.
1834.	,, Samuel, Dublin.		W.
1734.	,, William, Kilua, Co. Meath.		G.
1729.	**Charlemont,** Anne, Lady Viscountess.		W.
1726.	,, William, Viscount.		W.
1834.	**Charleton,** Elizabeth, spinster, Raphoe, Co. Donegal.		W.

IRISH WILLS: COPIES AND ABSTRACTS.

Date of Probate.		REFERENCE.
1727.	**Charlton,** Richard, merchant, Dublin.	W.
1707.	**Charters,** Henry, merchant, Lisburn, Co. Antrim.	W.
1834.	,, Rev. Mark, Ferns, Co. Wexford.	W.
1726.	**Chaucherie,** Clenet, Dublin.	W.
1727.	,, Sarah, widow, Dublin.	W.
1834.	**Cherry,** Robert, Drumherriff, Co. Armagh.	W.
1474.	**Chever,** John, Dublin.	T. & B., p.146.
1684.	**Chillam,** Patrick, alderman, Drogheda.	G.
1633.	,, Robert, alderman, Drogheda.	G.
1834.	**Christian,** Thomas, Subconstable of Police, Trim, Co. Meath.	W.
1707.	**Chudleigh,** Thomas, Kinsale, Co. Cork.	G.
1728.	**Clanchy,** George, Dublin.	W.
1728.	**Clanrickard,** Michael, Earl of	W.
1664.	,, Richard, Earl of	W.
1791.	**Clare,** Benjamin, Leixlip, Co. Kildare.	C.
1797.	,, Joshua, Claremont, Co. Meath.	C.
1650.	,, Thomas, merchant, Dublin.	C.
1777.	**Clark,** George.	W.
1834.	,, John, coachmaker, Bristol.	W.
1708.	,, Thomas, Ardress, Co. Armagh.	G.
1729.	,, William, merchant, Dublin.	W.
1752.	**Clarke,** Anne, Dublin.	G.
1834.	,, Denis, merchant, Galway.	W.
1777.	,, or **Clark,** Elizabeth, spinster, Dublin.	W.
1701.	,, Ellen, widow, Drogheda.	G.
1729.	,, Gabriel, Lisnalee, Co. Kilkenny.	W.
1727.	,, Henry, Anaghsamry, Co. Armagh.	W. & G.
1777.	,, Rev. Henry, D.D., Rector of Clonfecle, Co. Armagh.	W.
1706.	,, Humphrey, Ballinderry, Co. Antrim.	W.
1728.	,, Sir James, Kt., East Moulsey, Surrey.	W.
1691.	,, John, Portadown, Co. Armagh.	G.
1834.	,, Dr. Joseph, Dublin.	W.
1727.	,, Prudence, widow, Portadown, Co. Armagh.	W. & G.
1729.	,, Simon, Dublin.	W. & G.
1752.	,, Thomas, Ardress, Co. Armagh.	G.

IRISH WILLS: COPIES AND ABSTRACTS.

Date of Probate.		REFERENCE.
1834.	**Clarke,** Thomas, farmer, Kinnefad, King's Co.	W.
1726.	**Clayton,** John, Dean of Kildare.	W
1834.	,, John, merchant, Galway.	W.
1834.	**Clear,** James, Mountrath, Queen's Co.	W.
1777.	**Cleland,** James, Newtownards, Co. Down.	W.
1834.	,, Rev. John Armagh.	W.
1834.	,, or **Clieland,** Robert, Kilmore, Co. Down.	W.
1777.	**Clements,** Nathaniel, Rt. Hon. Privy Councillor, Dublin.	W.
1728.	,, Theophilus, Dublin.	W.
1727.	**Clervaux,** Hester, widow, Portarlington, Queen's Co.	W.
1728.	**Clibborn,** Joshua, Moate, Co. Westmeath.	W.
1729.	**Cliffe,** Anthony, Dungulph, Co. Wexford.	G.
1700.	,, Eleanor, widow, Dungulph, Co. Wexford.	G.
1691.	,, John, Dungulph, Co. Wexford.	G.
1727.	,, John, New Ross.	G.
1729.	,, Loftus, Blarney, Cork.	W. & G.
1834.	,, Mary, spinster, Walcot, Somerset.	W.
1666.	,, Robert, chirurgeon, Sandbach, Cheshire.	W. & G
1693.	**Clifford,** Joseph, Cork.	G.
1721.	**Clifton,** Arthur, Dublin.	G.
1656.	**Clinton,** James, Clintonstown, Co. Louth.	G.
1729.	,, Nicholas, gun-smith, Dublin.	W.
1678.	**Cloud,** John, yeoman, Knockmoura, Co. Cork.	G.
1777.	**Coates,** Thomas, Driminure.	W.
1707.	**Cockerill,** William, Cork.	W.
1645.*	**Cockman,** Francis, clerk, St. Patrick's, Dublin.	Y. Bandle. Nov. 1647-48.
1679.	**Cocks,** Sarah, widow.	G.
1728.	,, William, Ninch, Co. Meath.	W.
1777.	**Codd,** James, grocer, Bishop Street, Dublin.	W.
1696.	,, Loftus, Castletown, Co. Wexford.	G.
1728.	**Coddington,** Dixie, Holmpatrick, Co. Dublin.	W.
1834.	**Coffey,** John, merchant, Carlow.	W.
1834.	,, Patrick, hotel-keeper, Dublin.	W.
1695.	,, Thomas, clerk, Linally, King's Co.	N. Vol. 149. p.365.

IRISH WILLS: COPIES AND ABSTRACTS.

Date of Probate.		REFERENCE
1884.	**Cogan,** or **Keogan,** Patrick, farmer, Balgree, Co. Meath.	W.
1590.*	**Coghlan,** John, Fuire (Wheery).	D.
1726.	**Colclough,** Cæsar, Rosgarland, Co. Weford.	W.
1798	,, Sir Vesey, Bt., Tintern, Wexford.	M. v. XII, 463.
1729.	**Cole,** Richard, Lieut.-Col. in Sir J. Witherington's Regt.	W.
1762.	**Coles,** Samuel, Kildermod, Co. Wexford.	M. v. XII, 459.
1727.	**Colles,** Charles, Dublin.	W.
1709.	**Colley,** Christopher, Dublin.	G.
1768.	,, Dudley, Rahin, Co, Kildare.	G.
1760.	,, Elizabeth, Dublin.	G.
1743.	,, Frances, Dublin.	G.
1712.	,, George, Rahin, Co. Kildare.	G.
1688.	,, Gerard, apothecary, Drogheda.	W.
1687.	,, Sir Henry, Kt., Castle Carberry, Co. Kildare.	G.
1719.	,, Henry, alias **Cowley,** Castle Carberry, Co. Kildare.	G.
1759.	,, Henry, Rahin, Co. Kildare.	G.
1777.	,, John, Ballywalter, Co. Wexford.	W.
1764.	,, Mary, Castle Carberry, Co. Kildare.	G.
1746.	,, Sarah, Dublin.	G.
1646.	,, Sir William, Kt., Edenderry, King's Co.	G.
1884.	**Collier,** Matthew, farmer, Borranstown, Co. Dublin.	W.
1667.	**Collins,** John, Shankhill, Co. Kilkenny.	W.
1777.	,, John, Marlinstown, Co. Westmeath.	W.
1884.	,, John, farmer, Kilmeen, Co. Cork.	W.
1728.	**Collis,** John, Bannagh, Co. Kerry.	W.
1884.	**Colquitt,** John Scrope, Capt. in 1st Regt. of Foot Guards.	W.
1660.	**Colthurst,** John, late of Naas.	G.
1681.	,, John, Cooleneshanvally, Co. Cork.	G.
1804.*	,, John, Dripsey Castle, Co. Cork.	P.
1745.*	,, Nicholas.	G.
1755.	,, Nicholas, Ballyally, Co. Cork.	G.
1666.	**Comely,** John, Dublin.	W.
1728.	**Conar,** Dennis, merchant, Dublin.	W.
1884.	**Condon,** John, shop-keeper, Glanworth, Co. Cork.	W.
1884.	,, Richard, shop-keeper, Cork.	W.

IRISH WILLS: COPIES AND ABSTRACTS.

Date of Probate.		Reference.
1729.	**Conelly**, Rt. Hon. William.	G.
1666.	**Coningham**, James, Blarwhush, Scotland.	W.
1777.	**Connell**, Peter, Cranary, Co. Longford.	W.
1834.	**Connellan**, John, Dublin.	W.
1720.	**Conner**, Daniel, Bandon, Co. Cork.	C.
1808.	**Connolly**, Arthur, lime-burner, Dublin.	G.
1777.	**Connor**, Margaret, spinster.	W.
1834.	,, Owen, attorney, Dublin.	W.
1683.	,, Thady, Corbally, Co. Tipperary.	W.
1762.	**Conolly**, Rev. Arthur, Finglass, Co. Dublin.	G.
1729.	,, Rt. Hon. William, Dublin.	W.
1707.	**Conran**, William, merchant, Dublin.	W.
1777.	**Conry**, John, Pollymount, Co. Roscommon.	W.
1667.	**Consedine**, Captain Mathew.	W.
1726.	**Conyers**, Thomas, Catherlogh.	W.
1668.	**Conyngham**, or **Conningham**, Frances, widow.	W.
1706.	,, Brigadier Henry, Mountcharles, Co. Donegal.	W.
1834.	,, Henry, Marquis of.	W.
1777.	,, John, Captain in 92nd Regiment of Foot.	W.
1777.	**Cook**, Richard, Dublin.	W.
1666.	**Cooke**, Catharine, Dunshaughlin, Co. Meath.	W.
1667.	,, Edward, Dublin.	W.
1727.	,, George, Fethard, Co. Tipperary.	W.
1708.	,, John, Kiltynane, Co. Tipperary.	W.
1706.	,, Peter, Carrick.	W.
1707.	,, Phanuel, Garrangibbon, Co. Tipperary.	W.
1706.	,, Thomas, merchant, Cork.	W.
1726.	,, Thomas, Dublin.	W.
1763.*	,, Rev. Thomas, Middleton School, Co. Cork.	G.
1707.	**Cooley**, John, Lisheen, Co. Tipperary.	W.
1777.	**Cooper**, James, Mary's Lane, Dublin.	W.
1834.	,, Mary, Rathfarnham, Co. Dublin.	W.
1681.	**Coote**, Anne, widow, Killester, Co. Dublin.	W.
1697.	,, Chidley, son of Charles, 1st Earl Mountrath.	G.
1702.	,, Chidley, Kilmallock, Co. Limerick.	G.

IRISH WILLS: COPIES AND ABSTRACTS.

Date of Probate.		REFERENCE.
1719.	**Coote,** Chidley, Dublin.	G.
1834.	,, Eyre, West Park, Rockbourne, England.	W.
1777.	,, Margaret, widow, Dublin.	W.
1744.	**Copley,** Anthony, Newcastle, Co. Limerick.	G.
1758.	,, John, Cork.	G.
1673.	,, Mary, alias **Chichester,** widow, Dublin.	G.
1473.	**Cor,** John, Dublin.	T. & B., p.57.
1777.	**Corcoran,** Catherine, alias **Lawler,** widow, Dublin.	W.
1834.	**Cordeal,** Marcella, spinster, Cloughan, Co. Longford.	W.
1834.	**Corken,** Rev. John, Aghalee, Co. Antrim.	W.
1780.	**Corker,** Alice, Cork.	C.
1748.	,, Chambre, Falmouth and Dublin.	C.
1790.	,, Chambre, archdeacon, Upper Lota, Cork.	C.
1845.	,, Chambre, Cor. Castle, Co. Cork.	C.
1755.	,, Daniel, King's Street, Oxmanstown.	C.
1733.	,, Colonel Edward, Ballymaloe, Co. Cork.	C.
1781.	,, Edward, Dublin.	C.
1720.	,, Esther, widow, Dublin.	C.
1789.	,, James Chambre, St. Buryan, Cornwall.	C.
1651.*	,, John, merchant, Dublin.	C.
1772.	,, Joseph, St. Buryan, Cornwall.	C.
1790.	,, Martha, spinster, Dublin.	C.
1739.	,, Rebecca, spinster, Dublin.	C.
1765.	,, Robert, LL.D., St. Buryan, Cornwall.	C.
1770.	,, Robert, St. Buryan, Cornwall.	C.
1772.	,, Ruth, widow, Dublin.	C.
1737.	,, Thomas, merchant, Dublin.	C.
1777.	,, Thomas, Cork.	C.
1834.	**Corocan,** Daniel, farmer, Dairy Farm, Co. Kildare.	W.
1834.	**Corrigan,** John, Dublin.	W.
1834.	,, Thomas, seedsman, Dublin.	W.
1834.	**Corry,** Rev. Isaac Marcus.	W.
1834.	**Cosgrave,** Michael, farmer, Moyvalley, Co. Kildare.	W.
1744.	**Cossart,** Peter, merchant, Cork.	G.
1784.	,, Peter, merchant, Cork.	G.

IRISH WILLS: COPIES AND ABSTRACTS.

Date of Probate.		REFERENCE.
1728.	**Cossens,** George, inn-keeper, Ballymaddock, Queen's Co.	W.
1834.	**Costello,** Martin, shop-keeper, Ennis, Co. Clare.	W.
1834.	**Costeloe,** Thomas, Eyre Court, Co. Galway.	W.
1631.*	**Cottell,** Walter, New Ross, Co. Wexford.	G.
1706.	**Coulter,** Andrew, Clonmel, Co. Tipperary.	W.
1788.	**Court,** Mary, widow.	G.
1698.	,, Richard, glazier, Belfast.	G.
1701.*	,, Richard.	G.
1728.	,, William, peruke-maker, Dublin.	W. & G.
1710.	**Courtenay,** George, Ballytrasny, Co. Cork.	G.
1791.	,, George, Midleton, Co. Cork.	G.
1782.	,, Maurice, Midleton, Co. Cork.	G.
1727.	**Cousser,** John Sigismond, Dublin.	W.
1707.	**Coutlers,** Lieut. Augustine de.	W.
1834.	**Cowan,** Andrew, Ballylintogh, Co. Down.	W.
1777.	**Cowney,** Roger, merchant, Limerick.	W.
1761.	**Cox,** Ann, widow.	G.
1777.	,, Deborah, widow, Inch, Co. Cork.	G.
1664.	,, Jasper, alderman, Youghal, Co. Cork.	W. & G.
1766.	,, John, Coolkirky, Co. Cork.	G.
1650.	,, Capt. Richard.	G.
1731.	,, Richard, Dunmanway, Co. Cork.	G.
1834.	,, Rev. Richard, Cahirconlish Glebe, Co. Wicklow.	W.
1650.	,, Robert, merchant, Youghal, Co. Cork.	G.
1730.	,, Susanna, widow, Ardlandstown, Ballymartle, Co. Cork.	G.
1732.	,, Thomas, Coolkirky, Co. Cork.	G.
1728.*	,, William, Ardlandstown, Co. Cork.	G.
1791.	**Coyne,** Anne, alias **Eccles,** widow, Ballyshannon, Co. Donegal.	N. v. 150, p.132.
1834.	**Crampton,** John, Sidmouth, Co. Dublin.	W.
1834.	**Cransten,** William, Corwillis, Co. Cavan.	W.
1834.	**Crawford,** Cooper, Dublin.	W.
1777.	,, Hugh, merchant, Carlingford, Co. Louth.	W.
1707.	,, Thomas, New Ross, Co. Wexford.	W.
1834.	,, William, Portarlington, Queen's Co.	W.
1726.	**Creagh,** James, merchant, Limerick.	W.

IRISH WILLS: COPIES AND ABSTRACTS.

Date of Probate.		REFERENCE.
1834.	**Creed,** Rebecca, widow, Newcastle, Co. Limerick.	W.
1728.	**Creichtown,** Major-General David.	W.
1834.	**Creighton,** Rt. Hon. Lady Catherine, spinster, Dublin.	W.
1664.	**Cressey,** George, Dublin.	W.
1729.	**Crilly,** John, Kilcurry, Co. Louth.	W.
1728.	**Cripps,** Elias, merchant, Dublin	W.
1473.	**Cristore,** Jonet, alias **Fox.**	T. & B., p.56.
1834.	**Crofton,** Rev. Henry, Kilmainham.	W.
1834.	,, Sir Hugh, Bart., Mohill, Co. Leitrim.	W.
1706.	,, James, capt. in Lord Dungannon's Regiment of Foot.	W.
1834.	,, Marcia Anastasia, widow, Inchinappa, Co. Wicklow.	W.
1718.*	**Crofts,** George, Velvestown, Co. Cork.	G.
1730.*	,, George, Churchtown, Co. Cork.	G.
1741.	,, Mary, widow, Churchtown, Co. Cork.	G.
1730.	,, Philip, Cork.	G.
1834.	,, Richard, merchant, Cork.	W.
1724.*	,, Roger, Knockbarry, Co. Cork.	G
1834.	**Croghan,** Mary, spinster, Galway.	W.
1726.	**Croker,** Richard, Nadrid, Co. Cork.	W.
1728.	**Crommelin,** Lewis, Lisburn Co. Antrim.	W
1726.	,, Samuel, Lisburn, Co. Antrim.	W.
1661.	**Cromwell,** Lord, Ardglass.	W.
1727.	**Cronyn,** William, Sledy, Co. Waterford.	W.
1814.	**Crookshank,** Alexander, Justice of Court of Common Pleas.	G.
1826.	,, Esther, Bath.	G.
1728.	**Crossthwait,** William, druggist, Dublin.	W.
1777.	**Crothers,** James, Ballydown, Co. Down.	W.
1834.	,, John, merchant, Blackwatertown, Co. Armagh.	W.
1726.	**Crow,** Charles, Bishop of Cloyne.	W.
1777.	,, Mary, alias **Baldwin,** widow, Tullamore, King's Co.	W.
1706.	**Crozer,** John, Cavan.	W.
1834.	**Crozier,** Frances Mary Anne, widow, Killyleagh, Co. Down.	W.
1834.	,, William, Dublin.	W.
1834.	**Cruise,** William Piers, Dublin.	W.
1727.	**Cuffe,** Agmondisham, Desart, Co. Kilkenny.	W.

IRISH WILLS: COPIES AND ABSTRACTS.

Date of Probate.		REFERENCE.
1777.	**Cuffe,** Catherine, widow, Dublin.	W.
1777.	,, Joseph, Blackrock, Co. Dublin.	W.
1729.	**Cullen,** George, merchant, Thurles, Co. Tipperary.	W.
1834.	**Cuming,** George, grocer, Drumbo, Co. Down.	W.
1777.	**Cummin,** John, lieut. in the Blue Horse.	W.
1834.	**Cummins,** John, barrister, Dublin.	W.
1777.	**Cuningham,** Francis, Ellis Quay, Dublin.	W.
1667.	,, James, Ballyachon, Co. Down.	W.
1727.	,, Robert, capt. in Royal Fusiliers.	W.
1683.	**Cuppage,** Robert, Lambstown, Co. Wexford.	W.
1666.	,, Stephen, alderman, Coleraine.	W.
1726.	**Cuppaidge,** Faustin, Dublin.	W.
1834.	**Curtis,** Anne, spinster, Dublin.	W.
1726.	,, Robert, Island Bridge, Dublin.	W.
706.	,, Thomas, Flemonstown Co. Meath.	W.
726.	**Curwen,** Elizabeth, widow, Chepilizod, Co. Dublin.	W.
1706.	**Cusack,** Francis, Killballyporter, Co. Meath.	W.
1777.	,, Joseph, merchant, Ennis, Co. Clare.	W.
1777.	,, Marrin, alias **Brownly,** widow.	W.
1681.	**Cusaoke,** Adam, Jus. Com. Pleas., Rathgar, Co. Dublin.	W.
665.	,, James, Dublin.	W.
834.	**D'Abbadie,** Arraud Michael, Paris	W.
1682.	**Dale,** Thomas, tailor, Dublin.	W.
727.	**Dalton,** Isaac, Athy, Co. Kildare.	W.
834.	**Daly,** Daniel, spirit dealer, Belfast.	W.
834.	,, Rev. Eugene, P.P., Colombhill, Co. Longford.	W.
777.	,, John, merchant, Mullingar, Co. Westmeath.	W.
707.	**Dalyell,** Thomas, Ticknevan, Co. Kildare.	W.
777.	**Dancer,** Sir Thomas, Bart., Modercany, Co. Tipperary.	W.
707.	**Dancey,** Paul, Rathrenoge, Co. Meath.	W.
729.	**Daniel,** George, yeoman, Donabate, Co. Dublin.	W.
834.	,, John, Clonmel, Co. Tipperary.	W.
834.	,, Nicholas Charles, Westbrooke, Dorset.	W.
777.	**Daniell,** Stennous, Carrickmacross, Co. Monaghan.	W.
476.	**Dansay,** Joan, alias **Duff,** Rowlestown.	T. & B. p.148.

IRISH WILLS: COPIES AND ABSTRACTS.

Date of Probate.			REFERENCE.
1834.	**Darby,** John, Westminster.		W.
1666.	**Darcy,** Dominick, Clonvane, Co. Clare.		W.
1728.	,,	Dominick, Knockane, Co. Clare.	W.
1708.*	**Daunt,** Achilles, Tracton Abbey, Co. Cork.		G.
1756.*	,,	Achilles, Gortigrenane, Co. Cork.	G.
1768.	,,	Elizabeth, Gortigrenane, Co. Cork.	G.
1785.	,,	Emmanuel, Kinsale, Co. Cork.	G.
1722.	,,	Francis, senr., Knockatoure, Co. Cork	G.
1747.	,,	Francis, Ballingarry, Co. Cork.	G
1733.	,,	George Nohovall, Co. Cork.	G.
1739.	,,	Henry, Fahalea, Co. Cork.	G.
1741.	,,	Henry, Dublin.	G
1680.	,,	Jane, widow, Tracton Abbey, Co. Cork.	G
1710.	,,	Martha, widow, Gortigrenane, Co. Cork.	G
1733.	,,	Mary, widow, Knockatore, Co. Cork.	G
1762.	,,	Mary, Cork.	G.
1765.	,,	Samuel, Willowhill, Co. Cork.	G.
1761.	,,	Swithin, chandler, Cork.	G
1670.	,,	Thomas, Owlpen, Glos.	G
1754.	,,	Thomas, carpenter, Cork.	G
1682.	,,	William, senr., Grillagh, Co. Cork.	G
1736.	,,	William, Willowhill, Co. Cork.	G
1768.	,,	William, Ballyverane, Co. Cork.	G
1732.	**Davenport,** Thomas, apothecary, Ennis, Co. Clare.		G
1748.	,,	Thomas, apothecary, Ennis, Co. Clare.	G
1784.	,,	Thomas, Askeaton, Co. Limerick.	G
1728.	**Davey,** Joseph, merchant, Londonderry.		W
1727.	,,	Samuel, merchant, Londonderry.	W.
1834.	**Davies,** Edward, wax-chandler, Cork.		W.
1727.	**Davis,** David, burgess, Limerick.		W.
1726.	,,	Dudley, Dublin.	W.
1708.	,,	Henry, Carrickfergus.	W.
1777.	,,	or **Dories,** Jeffrey, Clonfenoge, Co. Galway.	W.
1667.	,,	John, Dublin.	W.
1706.	,,	John, brewer, Island Bridge, Dublin.	W.

IRISH WILLS: COPIES AND ABSTRACTS.

Date of Probate.		REFERENCE.
1727.	**Davis,** Margaret, widow, Ballinekilbeg, Co. Carlow.	W.
1728.	,, Martha, widow, Dublin.	W.
1834.	,, Robert, breeches-maker, Piccadilly, London.	W.
1729.	,, William, Dublin.	W.
1728.	**Davison,** George, pewterer, Dublin.	W.
1666.	**Davoren,** Elizabeth, alias **Dutton,** widow, Dublin.	W.
1691.	**Dawley,** Edward, Little Island, Cork.	G.
1694.	,, Henry, Ballydaheene, Co. Cork.	G.
1681.*	,, Walter, Donnonstown, Co. Cork.	G.
1741.	**Dawly,** Dennis, Ballynookerry, Co. Cork.	G.
1653.	,, Elizabeth, widow, Macromp, Co. Cork.	G.
1735.	,, John, gardener, Cork.	G.
1750.	,, Thomas, Clounroben, Co. Cork.	G.
1834.	**Dawson,** Charles, Charlesfort, Co. Wexford.	W.
1780.*	,, Elizabeth, Cappagh, Co. Tipperary.	U.
1667.	,, John, late of Swaffham, Norfolk, now of Dublin.	W.
1777.	,, Rev. Joshua, Dublin.	W.
1756.	,, Moses, the elder, Gortnagragy, Co. Tipperary.	U.
1777.	,, Samuel, Rockcorry, Co. Monaghan.	W
1727.	,, Thomas, Dublin.	W.
1834.	,, Thomas, Moyallon, Co. Down.	W.
1834.	,, William, Lisnashanagh, Co. Down.	W.
1729.	**Day,** Robert, merchant, Dublin.	W.
1777.	**Dean,** Zachariah, fan-maker, Dublin.	W.
1726.	**Deane,** Elkanagh, Ballybeg, King's Co.	W.
1834.	,, Mary, spinster, Cork.	W.
1727.	,, Moses, Dublin.	W.
1707.	**Dease,** Oliver, merchant, Dublin.	W.
1834.	**Deey,** Catherine, spinster, Dublin.	W.
1666.	**De Geer,** Laurence, Lord of Osterby.	W.
1476.	**Delaber,** Nicholas.	T. & B., p.59.
1834.	**Delany,** Denis, Roskeen, Queen's Co.	W.
1834.	,, Peter, merchant, Drogheda.	W.
1834.	**De la Tour,** Paul Martin, Paris.	W.
1727.	**Delgarno,** Rev. William, Stewartstown, Co. Tyrone.	W.

IRISH WILLS: COPIES AND ABSTRACTS.

Date of Probate.

1834.	**Delvin,** Peter, Drogheda.	W.
1834.	**Denham,** Rev. Joseph, Killyshandra, Co. Cavan.	W.
1693.	**Denison,** John, Enniscorthy, Co. Wexford.	G.
1757.	**Dennis,** James, merchant, Cork.	G.
1745.	,, John, D.D., Diocese of Clogher.	G.
1707.	**Dennison,** Richard, Clonmel, Co. Tipperary.	W.
1673.	**Denny,** Sir Arthur, Kt., Tralee, Co. Kerry.	G.
1695.	,, Edward, Castle Lyons, Cork.	G.
1709.	,, Edward, Tralee, Co. Kerry.	G.
1834.	,, Sir Edward, Bart., Tralee Castle, Co. Kerry.	W.
1728.	,, John, Clonmel, Co. Tipperary.	W.
1666.	**Derenzi,** Frances, alias **Kean,** widow, Teens-Cross, King's Co.	W.
1727.	**Dermott,** Christopher, merchant, Dublin.	W.
1777.	**Desart,** Rt. Hon. Dorothy, Dowager Lady Baroness.	W.
1726.	**Deselaux,** Norah.	W.
1834.	**D'Esterre,** Letitia, Limerick.	W.
1728.	**De Villiers,** Samuel, quartermaster.	W.
1834.	**Devlin,** James, Creoghmoyola, Co. Derry.	W.
1726.	**Devonshire,** Christopher, merchant, Cork.	W.
1666.	**Dey,** Angeletta, widow, London.	W.
1665.	**Deyse,** Thomas, merchant, Drogheda.	W.
1777.	**Dickinson,** Daniel, merchant, Dublin.	W.
1777.	,, Richard, tanner, Dublin.	W.
1738.	**Dickson,** John, Ballybrickane, Co. Cork.	G.
1706.	,, Robert, Dublin.	W.
1834.	**Dignam,** Loughlin, carpenter, Celbridge, Co. Kildare.	W.
1834.	**Dillon,** Sarah, widow, Ballywilliam, Queen's Co.	W.
1682.	**Disney,** George, Stebannon, Co. Louth.	W.
1777.	,, Moore, Churchtown, Co. Waterford.	W.
1726.	**Dixon,** John, Allanswood, Co. Kildare.	W.
1729.	,, John, victualler, Ballimore, Co. Cork.	G.
1666.	,, Sir William, Kt., Dublin.	W.
1729.	**Dixson,** Angel, widow, Dublin.	W.
1696.*	**Dobbin,** Anthony, Gotladoc, Donegal.	G.
1714.*	,, Anthony.	G.

IRISH WILLS; COPIES AND ABSTRACTS.

Date of Probate.			REFERENCE.
1739.*	**Dobbin,** Charles.		G.
1748.	,,	Dorothy, widow of Maj. John Dobbin.	G.
1728.*	,,	Elizabeth, Goleduff, Co. Antrim.	G.
1757.	,,	Elizabeth, spinster, Drumkerrin, Co. Antrim.	G.
1772.	,,	Elizabeth, Rashee.	G.
1700.	,,	Hugh, Barrymagarachan, Co. Down.	G.
1731.	,,	Isabella.	G.
1682.	,,	James, Dumlane, Co. Antrim.	G.
1718.	,,	James, Inishrush, Co. Londonderry.	G.
1757.	,,	James, M.D., Carrickfergus.	G.
1740.	,,	John, capt., Dublin.	G.
1741.	,,	John, weaver, Belfast.	G.
1751.	,,	John, Edenderry, Co. Down.	G.
1777.	,,	John, Moville.	G.
1713.	,,	Moses.	G.
1733.	,,	Peter.	G.
1756.*	,,	Rigby.	G.
1733.	,,	Stephen.	G.
1673.	,,	Thomas, Drumsook, Co. Antrim.	G.
1687.	,,	Thomas, Carrickfergus.	G
1718.	,,	Thomas, Eskeleane, Co. Antrim.	G.
1703.	,,	William, burgess, Carrickfergus.	G
1722.	,,	William.	G.
1728.	,,	William, Dromore.	G.
1754.	,,	William, wheelwright, Belfort.	G.
1834.	**Dobson,** William, Moygannon, Co. Down.		W.
1708.	**Dod,** Paul, Galway.		W.
1707.	**Dodwell,** or **Dowdell,** Henry, Athlone, Co. Roscommon.		W.
1834.	,,	Roger, Mt. Dowdell, Co. Sligo.	W.
1791.	**Doherty,** Abigail, widow, Dublin.		G.
1756.	,,	James, Oldtown, Co. Tipperary.	G.
1759.	,,	Rev. James, Myros, Co. Cork.	G.
1715.	,,	Rev. John, Cashel.	G.
1787.	,,	John, Dublin.	G
1800.	,,	John, Middleton, Co. Dublin.	G.

IRISH WILLS: COPIES AND ABSTRACTS.

Date of Probate.		REFERENCE.
1834.	**Doherty,** John, Dublin.	W.
1788.*	,, . Margaret, widow, Cork.	G.
1810.*	,, Mary, widow, Cork.	G.
1765.	,, Samuel, Coolnaconnaught, Co. Cork.	G.
1834.	**Dollard,** Catherine, spinster, Rush, Co. Dublin.	W.
1729.	**Dolon,** Dominick, brewer, Dublin.	W.
1834.	**Dolphin,** Lieut. Gregory, Dortumna, Co. Galway.	W.
1774.	**Domville,** Rev. Benjamin, D.D., alias **Barrington.**	G.
1681.	**Donbavand,** Nathan, Warrington, Lancashire.	W.
1834.	**Donegan,** John, Bective, Co. Meath.	W.
1834.	**Donelan,** Honoria, widow, Eastwell, Co. Galway.	W.
1727.	**Doneraile,** Arthur, Lord Viscount.	W.
1689.	**Dongan,** Edward, Kiltaghan, Kildare.	G.
1665.*	,, John, Possickstown, Co. Kildare.	G.
1627.	,, Sir Walter, Castletown, Kildrought, Co. Kildare.	G.
1666.	**Donnaldson,** Alexander, Lubitavish, Co. Antrim.	W.
1777.	**Donnellan,** Thomas, Athenry, Co. Galway.	W.
1834.	,, William Rochfort, Bathwick, Somerset.	W.
1777.	**Donogh,** John, Newhouse, Co. Louth.	W.
1865.	**Donohue,** John, Rossacor, Co. Cork.	C.
1773.	**Donovan,** Edward, Dublin.	G.
1834.	,, Henry, provision dealer, Dublin.	W.
1834.	,, James, Dublin.	W.
1768.	,, Richard, Enniscorthy, Co. Wexford.	G.
1683.	**Dooner,** Garrott, Dublin.	W.
1726.	**Dore,** William, Bantyre, Co. Cork.	W.
1749.	**Dorman,** Richard, Monygormy, Co. Cork.	G.
1666.	**Dormer,** Michael, New Ross, Co. Wexford.	W.
1667.	**Doughty,** John, inn-keeper, Mary's Abbey, Oxmantown, Co. Dublin.	W.
1834.	**Douglass,** Rev. Charles, Dervock, Co. Antrim.	W.
1666.	**Dowdall,** Edward, Monktown, Co. Meath.	G.
1697.	,, Jane, widow, Dublin.	G.
1834.	,, John, Dublin.	W.
1706.	,, Margaret, spinster, Dublin.	W.
1729.	**Dowden,** Christopher, linen-weaver, Bandon, Co. Cork.	G.

IRISH WILLS: COPIES AND ABSTRACTS.

Date of Probate.		REFERENCE.
1832.	**Dowden,** Christopher, merchant, Bandon, Co. Cork.	G.
1847.	,, George, Bandon, Co. Cork.	G.
1785.	,, Joseph, merchant, Bandon, Co. Cork.	G.
1846.	,, Mary, widow, Bandon, Co. Cork.	G.
1682.	**Dowding,** Thomas, Dublin.	W.
1717.	**Dowe,** Anne, Coolerowe, Co. Cork.	G.
1723.	,, Isaac, Melane, Co. Cork.	G.
1714.	,, Joshua, Coolerowe, Co. Cork.	G.
1617.	,, Richard, Carrigrohane, Co. Cork.	G.
1789.	,, William, Tierelteen, Co. Cork.	G.
1728.	**Dowglass,** John, capt.-lieut. in Col. Howard's Regt. of Foot.	W.
1727.	,, Robert, a minor, Dublin.	W.
1682.	**Dowlen,** James, merchant, Youghal, Co. Cork.	W.
1834.	**Dowling,** Patrick, miller, Dublin.	W.
1834.	,, Walter Blake, Cararoe, Co. Galway.	W.
1707.	**Downes,** Elizabeth, wife of Dive, Bishop of Cork and Ross.	W.
1777.	,, Henrietta, Donnybrook, Co. Dublin.	W.
1708.	**Downing,** Richard, Lismore, Co. Waterford.	W.
1834.	**Downy,** Francis, Birr, King's Co.	W.
1727.	**Doyle,** Catherine, alias **Cruise,** widow, Aghvana, Co. Wicklow.	W.
1707.	,, Denis, farmer, Ballymacar, Co. Waterford.	W.
1834.	,, Elizabeth, widow, Dublin.	W.
1834.	,, Mary, spinster, Ballytore, Co. Kildare.	W.
1834.	,, Mary, Bishop's Court, Co. Kildare.	W.
1834.	,, Michael, farmer, Ballyfad, Co. Wexford.	W.
1778.	,, Thomas, plumber, Dublin.	G.
1777.	**Doyne,** Charles, V. Rev. Dean of Leighlin.	W.
1777.	**Drake,** Darius, Waterford.	W.
1834.	**Draper,** James, bookseller, Dublin.	W.
1668.	,, John, draper, Ballymodan, Co. Cork.	G.
1765.	,, John, linen-weaver, Cork.	G.
1770.	,, Mark, merchant, Cork.	G.
1784.	,, Samuel, Cork.	G.
1731.*	,, Sarah, Dublin.	G.
1642.	,, William, Bandon, Cork.	G.

IRISH WILLS: COPIES AND ABSTRACTS.

Date of Probate.		REFERENCE.
1784.	**Dreaper,** Joseph, Cork.	G.
1708.	,, Rachel, spinster, Kinsale, Co. Cork.	G.
1763.	**Drescoll,** Elinor, spinster, Dublin.	G.
1802.	**Drinan,** Andrew.	G
1788.	,, Lieut. Thomas.	G.
1831.	,, William Barry, Kilgobbin, Co. Cork.	G
1774.	**Drinane,** David, farmer, Knocknamanna, Co. Cork.	G
1759.	**Dring,** Robert, Cork.	G
1721.	,, Simon, Cork.	G
1834.	,, Simon, Rockgrove, Co. Cork.	W.
1757.	**Driscoll,** Elinor, widow, Limerick.	G.
1671.	,, John, Cork.	G.
1684.	,, Mary Ne Teige, Cork.	G
1750.	,, Rev. Thomas, Kilkenny.	G
1727.	**Drogheda,** Henry, Earl of.	W.
1666.	**Dromgoole,** Thomas, merchant, Dublin.	W.
1683.	**Dromore,** Essex Digby, Bishop of.	W.
1834.	**Drought,** Mary Anne, spinster, Ballyboy, King's Co.	W.
1726.	,, Robert, Park, King's Co.	W.
1834.	,, Robert, doctor, Durrow, Co. Kilkenny.	W.
1834.	**Druitt,** Joseph, Lisburn, Co. Antrim.	W.
1834.	**Drummond,** Michael, Kilmainham, Co. Dublin.	W.
1777.	**Drury,** Mary, widow, Dublin.	W.
1789.	**Drynan,** Thomas, farmer, Farrenbrien, Co. Cork.	G.
1726.	**Drysdale,** Major Hugh, Churchill's Regt. of Dragoons.	W.
1475.	**Drywer,** Joan, alias **Yate,** Crumlin.	T. & B., p.150.
1719.	**Duant,** Francis, Willowhill, Co. Cork.	G.
1480.*	**Dublin,** John, Archbishop of.	T. & B., p.167.
1681.	,, John Parker, Archbishop of.	W.
1472.	,, Michael, Archbishop of.	T. & B., p.25.
1729.	,, William King, Archbishop of	W.
1729.	**Ducasse,** Paschal, Dean of Clogher.	W.
1777.	**Dudley,** John, Raheny, Co. Dublin.	W.
1664.	**Duffe,** Edward, merchant, Dublin.	W.
1777.	**Dumaresq,** Anne, widow, Dublin.	W.

IRISH WILLS: COPIES AND ABSTRACTS.

Date of Probate.		REFERENCE.
1834.	**Dunbavin,** Frances, widow, Dublin.	W.
1834.	,, William, tallow-chandler, Dublin.	W.
1707.	**Dungannon,** Marcus, Lord Viscount.	W.
1834.	**Dunn,** Rev. William, Charleville, Co. Cork.	W.
1834.	**Dunning,** David, publican, Athlone, Co. Westmeath.	W.
1750.*	**Dunscombe,** George, Cork.	G.
1834.	,, Jane, widow, Cork.	W.
1740.*	,, Noblett, Mount Desart, Cork.	G.
1744.	**Dupleacks,** George, Edenderry, King's Co.	G.
1747.	,, Thomas, Edenderry, King's Co.	G.
1727.	**Du Verrier,** Captain Alexander, Dublin.	W.
1834.	**Dwyer,** Daniel, Dublin.	W.
1639.	**Dyer,** John, Knockroe, Cork.	G.
1757.	,, Sarah, Cork.	G.
1722.	,, Thomas, Baltimore, Co. Cork.	G.
1735.	,, Thomas, clothier, Cork.	G.
1690.	**Dymond,** Elizabeth, widow, Cork.	G.
1834.	**Eager,** William, Blessington, Co. Wicklow.	W.
1762.	**Earberry,** Christopher, Shandangin, Co. Cork.	G
1729.	**Earbery,** Mathias, Ballincollig, Co. Cork.	W.
1730.	,, Mathias, Ballincollig, Co. Cork.	G.
1779.	,, Mathias, Dublin.	G.
1729.	,, Nicholas, Ballincollig, Co. Cork.	W. & G.
1777.	**Eason,** Mary, widow, Cork.	W.
1834.	**Eastwood,** Francis, Falmore, Co. Louth.	W.
1682.	,, John, alderman, Dublin.	W.
1728.	**Eaton,** John, Castle Kelly, Co. Kilkenny.	W.
1665.	,, Richard, servant to Col. Thomas Longe	W.
1762.	**Eburn,** William, merchant, Cork.	G.
1750.	**Eccles,** Daniel, Fintonagh, Co. Tyrone.	N. Vol. 150, p.130.
1757.	,, Daniel.	G.
1793.*	,, Daniel, Tullymorris, Co. Fermanagh.	N. Vol. 150, p.130.
1697,	,, Elizabeth, widow, Dublin.	G.
1728.	,, Lady Elizabeth, Dublin.	G.

IRISH WILLS: COPIES AND ABSTRACTS.

Date of Probate.			REFERENCE.
1652.	**Eccles,** Francis, Dublin.		G.
1719.	,,	Gilbert.	G.
1680.	,,	Hugh, merchant, Belfast.	G.
1709.	,,	Hugh.	G.
1716.	,,	Hugh, Eccles Grove, Co. Wicklow.	G.
1747.	,,	Jane, widow, Belfast.	G.
1704.	,,	John, Malone.	G.
1726.	,,	John, Belfast.	W. & G.
1739.	,,	John, merchant, Belfast.	G.
1723.	,,	Joseph, Rathmoran, Co. Fermanagh.	G.
1709.	,,	Joyce, Dublin.	G.
1706.	,,	Mary, alias **Yarner,** Dublin.	G.
1710.	,,	Mary, widow, Waterford.	G.
1755.	,,	Mary, alias **Lowry,** widow, Fintonagh, Co. Tyrone.	N. Vol. 150, p.130.
1763.	,,	Robert, Kilrusky, Co. Fermanagh.	G.
1713.	,,	Samuel, Roan, Co. Armagh.	G.
1688.	,,	William, Dundesarl, Co. Antrim.	G.
1715.	,,	William.	G.
1742.	,,	William, Shanock, Co. Fermanagh.	G.
1834.	,,	William, Kiltimon, Co. Wicklow.	W.
1728.	**Eccleston,** Mary, alias **Barlow,** widow, Dublin.		W.
1726.	**Eckersley,** Charles, Ballmullmore, Co. Meath.		W.
1707.	**Eclin,** Robert, Dublin.		W.
1727.	**Edgworth,** Sir John, Kt., Lisard.		W.
1834.	**Edie,** Edward, Strabane, Co. Tyrone.		W.
1664.	**Edsall,** Matthew, farrier, Dublin.		W.
1728.	**Edwards,** John, Oldcourt, Co. Wicklow.		W.
1726.	,,	Thomas.	W.
1834.	**Elgee,** Angel, widow, Dublin.		W.
1665.	**Eliott,** William, inn-keeper, Dublin.		W.
1804.	**Elliott,** Elinor, alias **Savage,** Saintfield, Co. Down.		G.
1729.	,,	John, Lowtherstown.	W
1788.	,,	James, inn-keeper, Saintfield, Co Down.	G.
1727.	**Elwood,** Joseph, Demallstown, Co. Meath.		W.

IRISH WILLS: COPIES AND ABSTRACTS.

Date of Probate.		REFERENCE.
1728.	**Emerson,** Erasmus, Paddock, Queen's Co.	W.
1761.	**End,** Michael, Cork.	G.
1704.	,, William, merchant, Cork.	G.
1728.	**England,** David, Lifford, Co. Clare.	W.
1834.	**English,** James, Drummond, Co. Down.	W.
1834.	**Ennis,** Andrew, Dublin.	W.
1834.	,, Jane, Mill Street, Lancaster.	W.
1834.	,, John, Oswestry, Shropshire.	W.
1707.	**Ennos,** John, farmer, Claristown, Co. Meath.	W.
1687.	**Erbery,** Elizabeth, widow, Cork.	G.
1728.	**Esdall,** James, hatter, Dublin.	W.
1670.	**Eustace,** Sir Maurice, Kt. Lord Chancellor of Ireland.	W.
1729.	**Evans,** Catherine, widow, Dublin.	W.
1708.	,, Edward, merchant, Dublin.	W.
1729.	,, Frances, widow, Dublin.	W.
1729.	,, Josias, glazier, Dublin.	W.
1834.	,, Mary, spinster, Dublin.	W.
1706.	**Evers,** John, merchant, Drogheda.	W.
1727.	**Exshaw,** Edward, merchant, Dublin.	W.
1834.	**Ewing,** George, Dublin.	W.
1707.	**Eyres,** Mary, widow, Waterford.	W.
1729.	**Fade,** Johan, capt. in Col. Dubourgay's Regt. of Foot.	W.
1727.	,, John, merchant, Dublin.	W.
1688.	**Fagan,** John, merchant, Waterford.	W.
1749.	**Faggetter,** Mary, spinster, Cork.	G.
1727.	**Falkiner,** or **Faulkner,** Daniel, merchant, Dublin.	W.
1766.	,, Mary, widow, Cork.	G.
1777.	**Falkner,** Mary, widow, Dolphin's Barn, Co. Dublin.	W.
1727.	**Fane,** Lady Elizabeth, widow, Westminster, Middlesex.	W.
1784.*	**Fanning,** Audley, Matsmount, Co. Derry.	N. Vol. 151, p.115.
1727.	**Fargher,** Charles, cooper, Dublin.	W.
1708.	**Farley,** Richard, Gurtemonagh, Co. Donegal.	W.
1819.	**Farmer,** Helen, Cork.	G.
1771.	,, Hovel, Dr. of Physic, Cork.	G.

IRISH WILLS: COPIES AND ABSTRACTS.

Date of Probate.			REFERENCE.
1739.	**Farmer,** James, Kilrush, Co. Clare.		G.
1686.	,,	Major Jasper, Pennsylvania.	G.
1715.	,,	Jasper, Ardevalane, Co. Tipperary.	G.
1697.	,,	John, Kilshinane.	G.
1735.	,,	John, mariner, Youghal, Co. Cork.	G.
1808.	,,	Martha, spinster, Cork.	G.
1724.	,,	Mary, widow, Youghal, Co. Cork.	G.
1691.	,,	Richard, Ardra, Cork.	G.
1781.	,,	Rev. Richard, Cork.	G
1749.	,,	Robert, Cork.	G.
1808	,,	Thomas, shopkeeper, Youghal, Co. Cork.	G.
1777.	**Farquhar,** Thomas, cordwainer, Limerick.		W.
1777.	**Farrell,** Charles, M.D., Usher's Quay, Dublin.		W.
1729.	,,	Edward, merchant, Dublin.	W.
1720.	,,	Fergus, Dublin.	G.
1732.	,,	Fergus, merchant, London.	G.
1777.	,,	Henry, Sligo, Co. Sligo.	W.
1682.	,,	James, Clonequin, Roscommon.	W.
1831.	,,	Margaret, spinster, Longford.	M. Vol. XII, 459.
1777.	,,	Richard, merchant, Dublin.	W.
1728.	,,	Thomas, Dublin.	W.
1777.	**Fay,** George, Richmond, Co. Limerick.		W.
1777.	**Fayle,** John, Killonan, Co. Limerick.		W.
1694.	**Fendall,** Elizabeth, widow, Brocklesby, Cork.		G.
1729.	**Fenn,** Edward, brewer, Cork.		W.
1709.	**Fennell,** Alexander, Manning, Co. Cork.		G.
1735.	,,	Blessing, widow, Youghal, Co. Cork.	G.
1665.	,,	Gerald, M.D., Dublin.	W. & G
1666.*	,,	Gowan Fitz-James, widow of John Butler.	G.
1738.*	,,	Hester, widow.	G.
1674.	,,	John, Mahon, Cork.	G.
1682.	,,	John, merchant, Cork.	G.
1710.	,,	John, Curraghivore, Co. Cork.	G.
1738.	,,	John, Ballymorely, Co. Limerick.	G.

IRISH WILLS: COPIES AND ABSTRACTS.

Date of Probate.			REFERENCE.
1741.*	**Fennell,** John, Youghal, Co. Cork.		G.
1744.*	,, John, Clonfaddy, Co. Waterford.		G.
1751.	,, John, Clonfaddy, Co. Waterford.		G.
1763.	,, Maurice, Pickerstown, Co. Waterford.		G.
1728.	,, Robert, Ballyquain, Co. Cork.		G.
1759.	,, William, gardener, Cork.		G.
1664.	**Fenton,** Sir Maurice, Bart., Mitchelstown, Co. Cork.		W. & G.
1667.	,,, Sir William, Kt. Mitchelstown, Co. Cork.		G.
1671.	,, Sir William, Bart., Mitchelstown, Co. Cork.		G.
1671.	,, Sir William, Kt., Mitchelstown, Co. Cork.		G.
1681.	**Fenwick,** Ann, Bandonbridge, Co. Cork.		G.
1786.	,, Margaret.		G.
1667.	**Fenwicke,** John, Clonmore, Co. Catherlogh.		W.
1665.	,, Joshua, Clonmore, Co. Catherlogh.		W.
1729.	**Ferguson,** Victor, M.D., Belfast.		W.
1606.*	**Ferrell,** Richard, Coleigh, Tipperary.		G
1728.	**Fetherston,** Thomas, Castlekearan, Co. Meath.		W.
1708.	**ffrench,** Patrick, Duras, Co. Galway.		W.
1726.	**Finch,** Edward, Kilcoleman, Co. Tipperary.		W.
1666.	**Finglasse,** Richard, Dublin.		W.
1726.	**Finigan,** William, Mucklin, Co. Kildare.		W.
1777.	**Finn,** Edmond, printer and bookseller, Kilkenny.		W.
1777.	,, Luke, Colloony, Co. Sligo.		W.
1750.	**Fisher,** Lancelot, Aughenamallagh, Co. Monaghan.		G.
1768.	,, Preston, Balsoon, Co. Meath.		G.
1739.	,, William, merchant, Dublin.		G.
1707.	**FitzGerald,** Augustine, Carron, Co. Clare.		W.
1727.	,, Ellenor, widow, Dublin.		W.
1663.	,, James, Cluony, Co. Clare.		W.
1664.	,, Sir John Fitz Edmond, Kt., Ballymaloe, Cork.		A., 1879-82, p.269.
1683.	,, John, Youghal, Co. Cork.		W.
1729.	,, John, Park Prospect, Co. Cork.		W.
1735.	,, Lawrence.		N. Vol. 149, p.25.
1706.	,, Richard, Scartmodeligoe, Co. Waterford.		W.

IRISH WILLS: COPIES AND ABSTRACTS.

Date of Probate.			REFERENCE
1667.	**FitzGerald,** Thomas, Rath M'Cartie, Co. Tipperary.		W.
1668.	,,	Thomas, Kilcromin, Queen's Co.	W.
1736.*	,,	Thomas, Ovidstown, Co. Kildare.	N. v. 149, p.25.
1716*	,,	William, Ballynard, Co. Limerick.	G.
1731.	,,	William, Lacharne, Co. Kerry.	G.
1608.	**Fitzgibbon,** Edmond, Mitchelstown, Co. Cork.		A., 1879-82. Pedigree of White Knight.
1796.	,,	Elizabeth, widow, Clonmell, Co. Tipperary.	A. 1876-78, 332.
1795.	,,	Gerald, Castlegrace, Co. Tipperary.	A.· 1876-78, 330.
1795.	,,	Maurice, Castlegrace, Co. Tipperary.	A. 1876-78, 329.
1769.	,,	Philip, Castlegrace, Co. Tipperary.	A. 1876-78, 328.
1666.	**Fitz Harris,** Richard, merchant, Dublin.		W.
1714.	**Fitz Maurice,** Raymond, Dublin.		G.
1711.	,,	William, Gullane, Co. Kerry.	G.
1475.	**Fitz Rery,** Marion, alias **Fleming.**		T. & B., p.155.
1471.	**Fitz Robert,** John, Rathmore.		T. & B., p.22.
1726.	**Flanagan,** Charles, Croghan, King's Co.		W.
1777.	,,	Peter, Phillipstown, King's Co.	W.
1777.	**Fleming,** Catherine, Ballincarrow, Co. Sligo.		W.
1729.	,,	John, Drogheda.	W.
1708.	**Flemynge,** Thomas, Lisnelong, Co. Cavan.		W.
1683.	**Fletcher,** John, ironmonger, Dublin.		W.
1777.	,,	John, Rathfarnham, Co. Dublin.	W.
1777.	**Flood,** James, Roper's Rest, Co. Dublin.		W.
1726.	,,	William, merchant, Dublin.	W.
1725.	**Folque,** Henry, Killavy, Co. Fermanagh.		M. Vol. XI, p.509.
1728.	**Fontaine,** James, clerk, Dublin.		W.
1712.	**Foord,** John, alderman, Limerick.		G.
1765.	,,	Nicholas, Limerick.	G.
1708.	,,	Thomas, Q.-M. in Brig. Cunningham's Regt. of Dragoons.	W.
1677.	**Foott,** George, Moyallow, Cork.		G.
1758.	,,	George, Kilvealaton, Co. Cork.	G.
1777.	**Forbes,** Catherine, spinster, Ballinacoarah, Co. Meath.		W.
1729.	,,	Lady Dorothy, daughter to the Earl of Granard.	W.

IRISH WILLS: COPIES AND ABSTRACTS.

Date of Probate.		REFERENCE.
1727.	**Forbes,** Elizabeth, widow, Tamlaght.	W.
1727.	,, Rev. Thomas, Vicar of Dunboyne, Co. Meath.	W.
1729.	**Ford,** Mathew, Dawson Street, Dublin.	W.
1726.	,, Robert, merchant, Dublin.	W.
1726.	**Fordice,** John, Antrim Town.	W.
1729.	**Forrest,** Catherine, widow, Dublin.	W.
1785.	**Forsayeth,** John, Archdeacon of Cork.	G.
1681.	**Forstall,** Luke, merchant, Dublin.	W.
1682.	,, Rev. Marcus, D.D., Dublin.	W.
1683.	,, Peter, Carrigtoniny, Co. Kilkenny.	W.
1659.	**Forster,** Rev. Richard, Baltrea, Co. Dublin.	N. Vol. 148, p.363.
1745.	,, William, mariner, Cork.	G.
1765.*	,, William, clothier, Cork.	G.
1667.	**Fortescue,** John, Glenavy, Co. Antrim.	W.
1708.	**Fotterell,** Thomas, Dublin.	W.
1728.	**Foukes,** Deborah, widow, Ratoath, Co. Meath.	W.
1726.	,, Ellen, Monastervan, Co. Kildare.	W.
1732.	**Foulke,** Elizabeth, widow, Strawhall, Co. Cork.	G.
1760.	,, William, Dublin.	G.
1731.	**Foulks,** George, inn-keeper, Cork.	G.
1709.	**Fowke,** Matthew, apothecary, Cork.	G.
1783.	,, Norcott, Cork.	G.
1727.	**Fox,** Anthony, Gloghotanny, King's Co.	W.
1726.	,, Henry, Graigue, Co. Tipperary.	W.
1729.	**Foxwist,** Joseph, fringe-maker, Dublin.	W.
1707.	**Foy,** Nathaniel, Bishop of Waterford.	W.
1665.	**Franck,** John, Dublin.	W.
1727.	**Freeman,** John, Kappanagoute, Co. Cork.	W.
1718.	,, Richard, Ballinguile, Co. Cork.	G.
1732.	,, William, Castlecow, Co. Cork.	G.
1777.	**Freke,** Sir John, Bart., Castle Freke, Co. Cork.	W.
1728.	,, Sir Percy, Bart.	W.
1729.	**French,** Arthur, Clonyquil, Co. Roscommon.	W.
1711.	,, James, alderman, Cork.	G.

IRISH WILLS: COPIES AND ABSTRACTS.

Date of Probate.			REFERENCE.
1789.*	**French,** Robert, Rahasane, Co. Galway.		M. Vol. XII, 162.
1777.	**Frend,** George, Creville.		W.
1683.	,,	Samuel, Carrickereely, Co. Limerick.	W.
1769.	**Fuller,** Abraham, linen-draper, Cork.		G.
1630.	,,	Anne, widow, Bandon Bridge, Co. Cork.	G.
1728.	,,	Elizabeth, widow, Lahinch, King's Co.	W.
1752.	,,	Elizabeth, widow, Limerick.	G.
1745.	,,	George, Cork.	G.
1766.	,,	Ralph, Old Castle, Co. Cork.	G.
1641.	,,	Richard, St. Finbarrys, Cork.	G.
1666.	,,	Robert, Kinsale, Co. Cork.	G.
1643.	,,	Thomas, yeoman, Bandon Bridge, Co. Cork.	G.
1687.	,,	Thomas, Inniskeen, Cork.	G.
1677.	,,	Lieut. William, Ballymodan, Co. Cork.	G.
1773.	,,	William, farmer, Middle Manch, Co. Cork.	G.
1775.	,,	William, Cork.	G.
1778.	,,	William, Dublin.	G.
1683.	**Furlong,** Bridget, spinster, Wexford.		G.
1475.	**Fynglas,** Thomas.		T. & B., p.153.
1707.	**Gage,** William, Garnvaghy, Co. Londonderry.		W.
1707.	**Gahan,** Daniel, Dublin.		W.
1777.	**Gallagher,** John, Aughgrand, Co. Leitrim.		W.
1474.	**Galliane,** Hugh, Dublin.		T. & B., p.86.
1707.	**Gallway,** Arthur, captain, Ballynetray, Co. Waterford.		W.
1445.	**Galwey,** Geoffrey, Limerick.		A. 1898, p.122.
1707.	**Galwith,** James, silk-thrower, Wentworth Street, Middlesex.		W.
1731.	**Gambell,** Elizabeth, Waterford.		G.
1741.	**Gamble,** Arthur, Waterford.		G.
1749.	,,	Elizabeth, Cork.	G.
1800.	,,	George, Cullinagh, Co. Waterford.	G.
1815.	,,	George, farmer, Cullinagle.	G.
1707.	,,	John, merchant, Strabane, Co. Tyrone.	W.
1724.	,,	John, Oldcourt, Co. Cork.	G.
1731.*	,,	John, Ballyromanes, Co. Cork.	G.
1750.*	,,	John, St. John's, Wexford.	G.

IRISH WILLS: COPIES AND ABSTRACTS.

Date of Probate.		REFERENCE.
1784.*	**Gamble,** John, Lisnagree.	G.
1791.*	,, John, Dublin.	G.
1793.	,, John, Brookville, Co. Dublin.	G.
1769.	,, Onesiphorus, St. John's Wexford.	G.
1777.	**Gannan,** Richard, farmer, Wardtown, Co. Meath.	W.
1729.	**Gardner,** Robert, Westminster, Middlesex.	W.
1726.	**Garstin,** Anne, widow, Dublin.	W.
1660.	,, Captain Symon, Drogheda.	W.
1777	**Gartside,** John, grocer, Kevinsport, Co. Dublin.	W.
1681.	**Gash,** John, Castle Lyons, Cork.	G.
1741.	,, John, junior, prisoner in Cork gaol.	G.
1712.	,, Margaret.	G.
1779.	,, Richard, farmer, Ballinvollion, Co. Cork.	G.
1777.	**Gaskell,** William, Malpas-street, Dublin.	W.
1777.	**Gaven,** William, Dublin.	W.
1729.	**Gavin,** Robert, linen-draper, Ballyrasheen, Co. Londonderry.	W.
1727.	**Gay,** John, Grangegorman-lane, Co. Dublin.	W.
1706.	**Gayton,** John, brewer, Dublin.	W.
1726.*	**Geale,** Benjamin, Lisnure, Co. Tipperary	G.
1729.	**Gee,** Anne, widow, Leap, King's Co.	W.
1777.	,, Dorothy, widow, Castletown, Co. Meath.	W.
1671.	**Geere,** William, London.	W.
1797.	**Geoghegan,** Ignatius, Soho Square, London.	C.
1727.	,, Kedagh, Carne, Westmeath.	W. & C.
1727.	,, William, Brackanagh, King's Co.	W. & C.
1777.	**Gernon,** Margaret, widow, Back Lane, Dublin.	W.
1729.	,, Patrick, periwigmaker, Dublin.	W.
1728.	**Gerrard,** Ellinor, alias **Geoghegan,** Dublin.	W.
1667.	**Ghest,** John, Dublin.	W.
1777.	**Gibbin,** Martha, spinster, Dublin.	W.
1732.	**Gibbings,** John, Garranes, Co. Cork.	G.
1721.	**Gibbon,** Robert, Kilworth, Co. Cork.	G.
1777.	**Gibbons,** Thomas, lace-weaver, Dublin.	W.
1729.	**Gibson,** Thomas, lieut. and adjutant in Col. Pocock's Regt.	W.
1777.	**Gibton,** Jeffrey, Dublin.	W.

IRISH WILLS: COPIES AND ABSTRACTS.

Date of Probate.			REFERENCE
1760.	**Gifford,** Henry, New Ross, Co. Wexford.		G.
1762.	,,	Nicholas, Ballysop, Co. Wexford.	G.
1736.	,,	Ravenscroft, New Ross, Co. Wexford.	G.
1727.	**Giles,** Richard, alderman, Youghal, Co. Cork.		W.
1777.	**Gilker,** Eneas, Ballyvarry, Co. Mayo.		W.
1721.	**Gill,** Katherine, widow, Lurgan, Co. Armagh.		G.
1833.*	**Gillespie,** Annabella, widow, Dublin.		G.
1761.	,,	Elizabeth, Comber, Co. Down.	G.
1785.	,,	George, Ballyloughan, Co. Down.	G.
1755.	,,	Hugh, Cherry Valley, Co. Down.	G.
1798.	,,	Hugh, Ballyloughan, Co. Down.	G.
1741.	,,	James, watchmaker, Gortalowry, Co. Tyrone.	G.
1750.*	,,	John, Tullyear, Co. Down.	G.
1787.	,,	Margaret, widow, Dublin.	G.
1785.	,,	Robert, Parsonstown, King's Co.	G.
1791.	,,	Robert, Donaghadee, Co. Down.	G.
1795.*	,,	Capt. Robert Rollo, 20th Dragoons.	G.
1797.	,,	Robert, Bellaghley, Co. Down.	G.
1777.	,,	William, Waringstown.	G.
1788.	,,	William, Cumber, Co. Down.	G.
1773.	**Gillespy,** John, stationer, Dublin.		G.
1787.	**Gilliland,** Robert, Standing Stone, Co. Antrim.		G.
1793.	**Gillman,** Benjamin, Kinsale, Co. Cork.		G.
1820.*	,,	Elizabeth, widow, Cork.	G.
1841.	,,	Elizabeth, widow, Crosshaven, Co. Cork.	G.
1840.	,,	Ellen, widow, Bandon, Co. Cork.	G.
1847.	,,	Frances, spinster, Cheltenham, Eng.	G
1793.*	,,	George Massey, Capt. 27th. Regiment of Foot.	G.
1724.	,,	Henry, Killneglary, Co. Cork.	G.
1765.	,,	Herbert, Shanacloyne, Co. Cork.	G.
1854.	,,	Herbert.	G.
1870.	,,	Herbert, Old Park, Co. Cork.	G.
1733.	,,	Heyward, St. Finbary's, Co. Cork.	G.
1818.	,,	Hill, Kinsale, Co. Cork.	G.
1852.	,,	Holmes.	G.

Date of Probate.			REFERENCE.
1804.	**Gillman,** James, Baltinbrack, Co. Cork.		G.
1847.	,,	James, Coolflugh, Co. Cork.	G.
1724.*	,,	John, Curryheene, Co. Cork.	G.
1746.	,,	John, Curryheene, Co. Cork.	G.
1770.	,,	John, Gurteen, Co. Cork.	G.
1781.	,,	John, farmer, Pluckanes, Co. Cork.	G.
1786.	,,	John, Ballinaboly, Co. Cork.	G.
1794.	,,	John, Bellrose, Co. Cork.	G.
1840.	,,	John, Mill Lane, Co. Cork.	G.
1850.	,,	John, shoemaker, Cork.	G.
1724.*	,,	Philip.	G.
1796.	,,	Richard, Bandon, Co Cork.	G.
1758.	,,	St. Leger Heyward, Curryhene, Co. Cork.	G.
1709.*	,,	Silvester.	G.
1679.	,,	Stephen, Curryheene, Co. Cork.	G.
1710.	,,	Stephen, Clasmartel, Co. Cork.	G.
1748.	,,	Stephen.	G.
1841.*	,,	Stephen, Barleyhill, Co. Cork.	G.
1856.*	,,	Thomas.	G.
1689.	**Gilman,** Bridget, widow, Ballymodan, Co. Cork.		G.
1690.	**Glanally,** Susanna, Baroness.		G.
1475.	**Glayne,** Thomas.		T. & B., p.28.
1777.	**Glenn,** William, Cahirneman, Co. Galway.		W.
1777.	**Glynn,** Mary.		W.
1706.	**Goddard,** Richard, capt. in Col. Lellington's Regt.		W.
1664.	**Godwin,** Alice, widow, Dublin.		W.
1664.	,,	Stephen, Dublin.	W.
1729.	**Goffe,** Jonas, chandler, Waterford.		W.
1472.	**Gogh,** John, Dublin.		T. & B., p.39.
1777.	**Gold,** George, dairyman, Dublin.		W.
1682.	**Golding,** Mary, alias **Luttrell,** widow, Dublin.		W.
1476.	**Goldynge,** Richard, Tobersool.		T. & B., p.122.
1728.	**Goodaker,** William, Dublin.		W.
1726.	**Goodbody,** Matthew, tallow-chandler, Dublin.		W.
1669.	**Goodman,** James, maltman, Marbeg, Co. Cork.		G.

IRISH WILLS: COPIES AND ABSTRACTS.

Date of Probate.			REFERENCE.
1777.	**Goodman,** John, Trim, Co. Meath.		W.
1729.	**Goodwin,** Timothy, Archbishop of Cashel.		W.
1681.	**Goodwyn,** Robert, East Grinstead, Sussex.		W.
1666.	**Gookin,** Robert, Courtmaschery, Co. Cork.		W.
1727.	**Goold,** Thomas, merchant, Dublin.		W.
1691.	**Gordon,** Capt. Alexander, Ardandraigh, Co. Longford.		M. Vol. XI, 370
1729.	,, Jane, widow, Dublin.		W.
1668.	,, John, Cullybacky, Co. Antrim.		W.
1727.	,, William, banker, Paris.		W.
1777.	**Gore,** Charles, Goresgrove, Co. Kilkenny.		W.
1729.	,, Henry, Sligo, Co. Sligo.		W.
1727.	,, Robert, Artarmon, Co. Sligo.		W.
1727.	**Gorges,** Henry, Summerseat, Co. Londonderry.		W.
1728.	,, Jane, widow, Dublin.		W.
1728.	,, Richard, lieut.-gen.		W.
1667.	**Gough,** William, Dunasa, Co. Clare.		W.
1707.	**Gould,** John, vintner, Dublin.		W.
1684.	**Grace,** John, Brittas.		A. Vol. 1858-5! p.319.
1708.	,, Oliver, Shanganagh, Queen's Co.		W.
1683.	**Graham,** Anthony, alias **Grimes,** corporal of Trim.		W.
1706.	,, Arthur, Tullygraham, Co. Monaghan.		W.
1667.	,, John, Ballinan, Queen's Co.		W.
1724.	,, John.		G.
1738.*	,, John, shopkeeper, Cork.		G.
1777.	,, John, Gt. George's St., Dublin.		W.
1683.	,, Pearce, burgess, Limerick.		W.
1729.	**Granard,** Catherine, Dowager Countess of.		W.
1706.	**Grantham,** James, clerk, Ardmaile, Co. Tipperary.		W.
1708.	**Granville,** Lord John of Potheridge.		W.
1707.	**Gratan,** Rev. Patrick, D.D., Belcamp, Co. Dublin.		W.
1728.	**Graves,** Samuel, yeoman, Castle Dawson, Londonderry.		W.
1682.	,, William, Ramullin, Co. Meath.		W.
1729.	**Gray,** James.		W.
1751.	,, John, merchant, Cork.		G.
1763.	,, Mary, Cork.		G.

IRISH WILLS: COPIES AND ABSTRACTS.

Date of Probate.		REFERENCE.
1698.	**Gray,** Terence, Ballymodan, Co. Cork.	G.
1748.	,, William, chandler, Cork.	G.
1726.	**Graydon,** Alexander, ensign.	W.
1777.	**Green,** Deborah, spinster, Limerick.	W.
1683.	,, Godfrey, Killmanahane, Co. Waterford.	W.
1728.	,, Jane, widow, St. Sepulchre's, Dublin.	W.
1777.	,, Joseph, Dublin.	W.
1682.	,, Marmaduke, Drumisklin, Co. Fermanagh.	W.
1721.	,, Simon, junior, Youghal, Co. Cork.	F., p.97.
1733.	,, Simon, burgess, Youghal, Co. Cork.	F., p. 95.
1727.	,, Robert, Belfast.	W.
1878.*	**Greer,** Alfred, Dripsey House, Co. Cork.	P.
1777.	,, Henry, linen-draper, Lurgan, Co. Armagh.	W.
1664.	**Greggs,** James, merchant, Raheen, King's Co.	W.
1664.	**Gregorry,** Giles.	W.
1726.	**Gregory,** William, tanner, Dublin.	W.
1708.	**Greville,** John, Nicholstown, Co. Kildare.	W.
1650.	**Grey,** John, lieut.-colonel.	G.
1745.	**Griffin,** Ann, widow, Dublin.	G.
1683.	,, Edward, Griffinstown, Co. Westmeath.	W.
1717.	**Griffith,** Richard, Dean of Ross.	G.
1666.	,, Robert, serjeant-at-law, Dublin.	W.
1707.	**Grinaway,** Christopher, Bandonbridge, Co. Cork.	W.
1726.	**Grourk,** Denis, merchant, Dublin.	W.
1729.	**Grove,** Joseph, Tipperary.	W.
1682.	,, Thomas, Castle Shanachan, Co. Donegal.	W.
1729.	**Grubb,** John, New Ross, Co. Wexford.	W.
1726.	,, Rebecca, alias **Thresser,** widow, Waterford.	W.
1667.	**Guilford,** Elizabeth, Countess of.	W.
1706.	**Guilloneau,** John Peter, Sieur de Maison Neave, France.	W.
1766.	**Gun,** Townsend, Rattoo, Co. Kerry.	G.
1615.	,, William, Limerick.	G.
1744.	**Gunn,** George, Carrigafoyle, Co. Kerry.	G.
1691.	,, William, Rattoo, Co. Kerry.	G.
1728.	,, William, Rattoo, Co. Kerry.	G.

IRISH WILLS: COPIES AND ABSTRACTS.

Date of Probate.			REFERENCE.
1707.	**Hackett,** Thomas, Thurles, Co. Tipperary.		W.
1707.	**Haddock,** John, Carranbane, Co. Down.		W.
1701.	,,	Joseph, britcher, Cork.	G.
1761.	,,	Joseph, Ballygroman, Co. Cork.	G.
1770.	,,	Mary, Ballygroman, Co. Cork.	G.
1718.	,,	Thomas, Ballygroman, Co. Cork.	G.
1766.	,,	Thomas, Cooledaniel, Co. Cork.	G.
1726.	**Halbridge,** John, Dromore, Co. Down.		W
1735.	**Hall,** Rev. John, D.D., Ardstragh, Co. Tyrone.		G.
1728.	,,	Joseph, Ballaghtobin, Co. Kilkenny.	W.
1777.	,,	Joseph, merchant, Athlone, Co. Westmeath.	W.
1799.	**Hallagan,** Samuel, Dublin.		G.
1681.	**Halley,** Michael, skinner, Dublin.		W.
1714.	**Hamilton,** Adam.		G.
1726.	,,	Alexander, Lisnatunny, Ardstraw.	G.
1740.	,,	Rev. Alexander, Moneyrea, Co. Down.	G.
1772.	,,	Alexander.	G.
1707.	,,	Andrew, Mulenard, Co. Donegal.	W.
1665.	,,	Archibald, Archbishop of Cashel.	W.
1694.	,,	Archibald, Crehanan, Co. Donegal.	G.
1777.	,,	Archibald, M.D., Dublin.	W.
1803.	,,	Audley, Eccles Green, Co. Tyrone.	G.
1667.	,,	Dame Beatrice, Manor Elliston, Co. Tyrone.	W.
1777.	,,	Catherine, spinster, Dublin.	W.
1666.	,,	Claudius, Laragh, Co. Wicklow.	W.
1727.	,,	Edward, merchant, Galway.	W.
1664.	,,	Dame Elizabeth, alias **Willoughby,** wife to Sir Francis Hamilton.	W.
1777.	,,	Francis, Newforge, Co. Down.	W.
1699.	,,	George, Co. Tyrone.	G.
1702.	,,	Rev. George, Devenish.	G.
1718.	,,	George.	G.
1724.	,,	George.	G.
1728.	,,	Hans, Frankford, Co. Armagh.	W.
1689.*	,,	Hugh, Donagheady, Co. Tyrone.	G.
1683.	,,	Isabell, Killgole, Co. Donegal.	W.

IRISH WILLS: COPIES AND ABSTRACTS.

Date of Probate.			REFERENCE.
1706.	**Hamilton,**	James, Bangor, Co. Devon.	W.
1708.*	,,	James, Court Hills, Co. Meath.	N. Vol. 150, p.295.
1711.*	,,	Rev. James, Ballygroffer.	N. Vol. 150, p.295.
1714.	,,	James.	G.
1717.	,,	James.	G.
1728.	,,	James, Ballinagarvey, Co. Antrim.	W.
1736.	,,	James.	G.
1746.	,,	James.	G.
1768.	,,	James, Mount Charles, Co. Donegal.	N. Vol. 150, p.294.
1773.	,,	James.	G.
1791.	,,	James Moore, Desertcreate, Co. Tyrone.	N. Vol. 150, p.294.
1849.*	,,	James, Fintra House, Co. Donegal.	N. Vol. 148, p.151.
1726.	,,	Jane.	G.
1727.	,,	Jane, widow.	G.
1695.	,,	John, late of Comemucklack.	G.
1703.	,,	John.	G.
1706.	,,	John Brownhall, Co. Donegal.	W.
1707.	,,	John, Edergoll, Co. Tyrone.	G.
1708.	,,	John, Carrowbeg, Co. Tyrone.	G.
1726.	,,	John.	G.
1761.	,,	John, Co. Tyrone.	G.
1765.*	,,	John, Tullycullion, Co. Tyrone.	G.
1778.	,,	John, Killiglassan, Co. Cavan.	G.
1741.	,,	Lettice, widow, Millburn, Co. Derry.	G.
1780.	,,	Lodwick, Mullaghdrinagh, Co. Cavan.	G.
1662.	,,	Patrick, merchant, Strabane.	G.
1776.	,,	Patrick, Garrison, Co. Fermanagh.	G.
1678.	,,	Robert, Clady.	G.
1692.	,,	Robert, Killeclunie, Co. Tyrone.	G.
1712.	,,	Robert.	G.
1736.	,,	Robert.	G.
1777.	,,	Robert, barrister-at-law, Dublin.	W.

IRISH WILLS: COPIES AND ABSTRACTS.

Date of Probate.			REFERENCE.
1778.	**Hamilton,** Robert.		G.
1789.	,,	Robert, Manor Hamilton, Co. Leitrim.	G.
1709.	,,	Thomas, Currenshegoe, Co. Monaghan.	G.
1792.	,,	Thomas, Dublin.	G.
1683.	,,	William, clerk, Cashel.	W.
1694.*	,,	William, Cornemucklagh, Co. Tyrone.	G.
1744.	,,	William, Killycoran, Co. Tyrone.	G.
1747.	,,	William, Beltrim, Co. Tyrone.	G.
1751.*	,,	William, Anglish, Co. Tyrone.	G.
1707.	**Hamlin,** Bartholomew, merchant, Drogheda.		W.
1729.	**Handcock,** Joseph, merchant, Dublin.		W.
1726.	,,	Thomas, Twyford, Co. Westmeath.	W.
1701.	**Handcocke,** William, Recorder of Dublin.		G.
1777.	**Hanigan,** Maurice.		W.
1728.	**Hanlon,** Phelim, inn-keeper, Dublin.		W.
1760.	**Hansard,** Frances, widow.		G.
1759.	,,	Francis.	G.
1666.	,,	John, clerk, Waterford.	A., 1870, p.327
1770.	,,	Judith, widow, Baltinglass, Co. Wicklow.	G.
1709.	,,	Mary, widow, Dublin.	G.
1749.	,,	Nicholas, Dublin.	G.
1749.	,,	Rev. Ralph, Baltinglass, Co. Wicklow.	G.
1759.	,,	Rev. Ralph, Castledermot.	G.
1620.	,,	Sir Richard, Kt., Lifford, Co. Donegal.	G.
1748.	,,	Richard, Atherdee.	G.
1777.	**Harden,** William, Borrisoleigh, Co. Tipperary.		W.
1666.	**Harding,** Arthur, yeoman, Rathcurah, Co. Carlow.		G.
1777.	,,	William, Clonlee, King's Co.	W.
1681.*	**Hardman,** Robert, Drogheda.		M. Vol. XII, 367.
1716.	**Hardy,** Arthur, Tinry Lane, Co. Carlow.		G.
1720.	,,	Edward, Ballybar, Co. Carlow.	G.
1716.	,,	Thomas, Tinry Lane, Co. Carlow.	G
1726.	**Harford,** Elizabeth, widow, Dublin.		W.
1697.	**Harmer,** William, Inner Temple, Co. Cork.		G.

IRISH WILLS: COPIES AND ABSTRACTS.

Date of Probate.		REFERENCE.
1666.	**Harrington,** Walter, Dublin.	W.
1723.	**Harris,** Joseph, Cork.	G.
1727.	,, Laugharne, Mountmellick, Queen's Co.	W.
1714.	,, Richard, tanner, Bandonbridge, Co. Cork.	G.
1731.	,, Robert, tyler, Cork.	G.
1670.	,, Stephen, Cork.	G.
1670.	,, Thomas, cordwayner, Kinsale, Co. Cork.	G.
1718.	,, Thomas, Bantry, Co. Cork.	G.
1761.	,, Thomas, farmer, Kinsale, Co. Cork.	G.
1775.	,, Thomas, Tullig, Co. Cork.	G.
1721.*	,, William, Ballyvoloone, Co. Cork.	G.
1728.	,, William, cooper, Kinsale, Co. Cork.	G
1727.	**Harrison,** Christopher, captain in Brigadier Newton's Regt. of Foot.	W.
1726.	,, Francis, Dublin.	W.
1683.	,, Michael, Marlea, Co. Antrim.	W.
1667.	**Harrisone,** Mathew, Dublin.	W.
1664.	**Harrold,** Thomas, merchant, Sixmilebridge, Co. Clare.	W.
1707.	**Hart,** Anne, alias **Cusack,** widow, Glastown, Co. Meath.	W.
1771.	,, Elizabeth, widow, Derry.	H., p.119.
1660.	,, George, Templemore.	H., p.104.
1705.*	,, George, Crosskerril.	H., p.106.
1758.	,, George, Kilderry, Co. Donegal.	H., p.109.
1827.	,, Georgina, widow, Ballymagard, Co. Derry.	H., p.114.
1832.	,, General G. V., Kilderry, Co. Donegal.	H., p.114.
1838.	,, Rev. G. V. Ledwick, Glenalla, Co. Donegal.	H., p.116.
1712.	,, Henry, Muff, Co. Donegal.	H., p.106.
1734.	,, Rev. Henry.	H., p.117.
1737.	,, Henry, merchant, Derry.	H., p.117.
1763.	,, Henry, alderman, Dublin.	H., p.119.
1796.	,, Henry, alderman, Dublin.	H., p.120.
1750.*	,, Job, Antigua.	H., p.118.
1755.	,, John, Wardstick, Co. Berks.	H., p.108.
1817.	,, John, Ballymagard, Co. Derry.	H., p.112.
1681.	,, Merrick, Crover, Co. Cavan.	H., p.105.
1664.	**Hartshorne,** Edward, Wicklow.	W.

IRISH WILLS: COPIES AND ABSTRACTS.

1706.	**Hartus,** Henry, captain in Lord Mahon's Regt. of Foot.	W.
1681.	**Hartwell,** Frances, widow.	G.
1727.	,, Joseph, burgess, Limerick.	G.
1666.	**Harvey,** Sir Peter, Kt., Dublin.	W.
1777.	,, Rose, widow, Londonderry.	W.
1728.	**Harwood,** Rev. Richard, Mountmellick, Queen's Co.	W.
1727.	**Hattin,** Jonathan, slater, Dublin.	W. & G.
1738.	**Haught,** John, clerk, Kilskoran, Co. Wexford.	G.
1808.	**Haughton,** Abigail, widow, Ballitore, Co. Kildare.	G.
1689.*	,, Arthur.	G.
1778.	,, Benjamin, Mullamast, Co. Kildare.	G.
1805.	,, Catherine, widow, Dublin.	G.
1685.	,, Ellenor, widow.	G.
1664.	,, James, Wexford.	G.
1786.*	,, James, farmer, Roskaw, Co. Wicklow.	G.
1793.	,, John, Clontarf, Co. Dublin.	G.
1785.	,, Jonathan, Ballitore, Co. Kildare.	G.
1783.	,, Joseph, Reban, Co. Kildare.	G.
1772.	,, Mary, alias **Smally,** Dunboe, Co. Derry.	G.
1761.	,, Priscilla.	G.
1788.	,, Richard, farmer, Coolacock, Co. Wicklow.	G.
1658.	,, Stephen.	G.
1778.	,, Susanna, spinster, Kinsale, Co. Cork.	G.
1738.	,, Thomas, London.	G.
1743.	,, Thomas, farmer, Roskath, Co. Wicklow.	G.
1778.	,, William, schoolmaster, Waterford.	G.
1776.	**Hawkes,** George, merchant, Cork.	G.
1753.	,, John, Mounteen, Co. Cork.	G.
1777.	**Hawkins,** Frances, widow, Killaloe, Co. Clare.	W.
1720.	,, Rev. John, Royal Hospital, Dublin.	W.
1707.	,, John, merchant, Cork.	W.
1688.	**Hawkshaw,** Thomas, Oxmantown, Co. Dublin.	W.
1726.	**Hay,** James, apothecary, Dublin.	W.
1726.	**Haydock,** Josias, Kilkenny.	W.
1808.	**Hayes,** Benjamin, Marble Hill, Co. Cork.	G.

IRISH WILLS: COPIES AND ABSTRACTS.

Date of Probate.		REFERENCE.
1753.	**Hayes,** Daniel, carpenter, Cork.	G.
1727.	,, John, merchant, Ballenyclack, Co. Wicklow.	W.
1476.	**Haylot,** Nicholas.	T. & B., p 128.
1728.	**Hays,** William, M.D., Limerick.	W.
1763.*	**Hea,** Stephen, Carrigane, Co. Cork.	G.
1774.	**Healy,** Jane, widow, Cork.	G.
1726.	**Hease,** Darby, farmer, Ballyhadane, Co. Limerick.	W.
1707.	**Heatley,** William, Dublin.	W.
1666.	**Heaton,** Richard, D.D., Dean of Clonfert.	W.
1682.	**Helsham,** Nathaniel, tanner, Dublin.	W.
1846.*	**Hely,** Eleanor, spinster, Scart Lodge, Co. Waterford.	C.
1752.	**Henderson,** James, linen-weaver, Cork.	G.
1777.	,, John, Fahuran, King's Co.	W.
1777.	**Hendley,** Roger, Ileclash, Co. Cork.	W.
1728.	**Henley,** Jane, widow, Dublin.	W.
1728.	**Henzey,** Joshua, merchant, Dublin.	W.
1666.	**Hepburne,** William, Londonderry.	W.
1777.	**Herbert,** Rev. Robert.	W.
1706.	**Herne,** John, Dublin.	W.
1777.	**Hewetson,** John, cutler, Dublin.	W.
1707.	**Hewett,** Catharine, widow, Dublin.	W.
1707.	**Hewston,** George, lieut. in Lord Dungannon's Regt. of Foot.	W.
1666.	**Heyden,** Richard, vintner, Dublin.	W.
1808.*	**Hickes,** Ann, Carrick-on-Shannon.	N. Vol. 148, p.130.
1776.	,, George, Creaghta, Co. Roscommon.	N. Vol. 148, p.129.
1780.	,, George, clerk, Bushey Park, Co. Roscommon.	N. Vol. 148, p.130.
1707.	,, John, Kilkannan, Co. Cavan.	W.
1766.	,, Richard, Creta, Co. Roscommon.	N. Vol. 148, p.129.
1808.	,, Richard, Creta, Co. Roscommon.	N. Vol. 148, p.130.
1802.	,, Thomas, Crea, Co. Roscommon.	N. Vol. 148, p.130.
1727.	**Hicks,** Peter, clerk, Lisduff, Co. Tipperary.	W.

IRISH WILLS: COPIES AND ABSTRACTS.

Date of Probate.   REFERENCE.

Date of Probate.		Reference.
1728.	**Higgins,** Francis, Archdeacon of Cashel.	W.
1726.	,, James, Dublin.	W.
1756.	**Higginson,** Thomas, Monyhere, Co. Wexford.	G
1476.	**Higley,** Peter, Dublin.	T. & B., p.130
1698.*	**Hill,** Adam, Co. Tyrone.	G.
1749.	,, Adam, farmer, Derrykeighan, Co. Antrim.	G.
1776.*	,, Adam, Ballymoney.	G.
1780.	,, Ann, widow, Hollyhill, Co. Cork.	G.
1665.	,, Arthur, Hillsborough, Co. Down.	W.
1740.	,, Elizabeth, Ballynabowly, Co. Cork.	G.
1773.	,, Rev. Hugh, D.D., Dublin.	G.
1735.	,, John, clothier, Cork.	G.
1737.*	,, John, clothier, Cork.	G.
1810.	,, Lancelot, Limerick.	G.
1754.	,, Mary, widow, Cork.	G.
1682.	,, Moses, Hill Hall, Co. Down.	W.
1688.	,, Robert, Carrickmacross.	G.
1708.	,, Robert, brewer, Dublin.	W.
1772.	,, Robert, Coolimurry, Co. Wexford.	G.
1718.	,, Sarah, widow, Cork.	G.
1655.	,, Thomas, trooper.	G.
1672.	,, Thomas, Dublin.	G.
1673.	,, Thomas, D.D., Kilkenny.	G.
1680.	,, Thomas, Coolegilly, Co. Cork.	G.
1691.	,, Thomas, merchant, Cork.	G
1702.	,, Thomas, clothier, Cork.	G
1710.	,, Capt. Thomas.	G.
1615.	,, William, merchant, Bristol.	G.
1640.	,, William, yeoman, Kilbrogan, Co. Cork.	G.
1667.	,, William, D.D., Finglas.	W.
1729.	**Hinde,** Martha, widow, Dublin.	W.
1688.	**Hiorne,** John, Athy.	W.
1729.	**Hird,** Leonard.	W.
1670.	**Hoare,** Abraham, Dublin.	G.
1709.	,, Edward, alderman, Cork.	M. Vol. XII. p.159.

IRISH WILLS: COPIES AND ABSTRACTS.

Date of Probate.		REFERENCE.
1730.	**Hoare,** Joseph, merchant, Cork.	G. & M. Vol. XI, p.512.
1741.	,, Joseph, merchant, Cork.	G.
1724.	,, Richard, Dublin.	G.
1764.	,, Robert, Cork.	G.
1715.*	**Hobson,** Mary, widow, Dublin.	G.
1726.	**Hodder,** William, Hoddersfield, Co. Cork.	W.
1755.	**Hodges,** George,Shanangolden, Co. Limerick.	G.
1750.	**Hodges,** William, Shanangolden, Co. Limerick.	G.
1760.	**Hodson,** Elizabeth, widow, Coolkenno, Co. Wicklow.	M. Vol. XII, 170.
1729.	,, Leonard, clerk, Ballinacor, Co. Westmeath.	W.
1777.	**Hoey,** James, printer, Dublin.	W.
1664.	,, Sir John, Kt., Cotlandstown, Co. Kildare.	W.
1728.	**Holland,** Hezekiah, alderman, Crossagalla, Co. Limerick.	W.
1666.	**Hollywood,** John, Artaine, Co. Dublin.	W.
1683.	**Holmes,** Robert, Clongery, Co. Kildare.	W.
1707.	,, Sampson, Crone-ne-horne, Co. Wicklow.	W.
1718.	,, Thomas, clerk, Dromnafinchin, Co. Cork.	G.
1708.	**Holroide,** Elizabeth, widow, Dublin.	W.
1706.	,, Isaac, merchant, Dublin.	W.
1471.	**Holtoun,** John.	T. & B., p.21.
1682.	**Homan,** John, Moate, Co. Westmeath.	W.
1706.	**Honohane,** John, Broghill, Co. Cork.	W.
1667.	**Hooker,** Charles, Dublin.	W.
1667.	**Hoole,** William, Lisburn, Co. Antrim.	W.
1627.	**Hoopes,** Robert, yeoman, Belhinche, Co. Armagh.	Y.Reg. Test.39, 192.
1777.	**Hopkins,** Stephen, merchant, Cork.	W. & G.
1662.	**Hore,** Edmund, merchant, Cork.	G
1681.	,, James, merchant, Dungarvan, Co. Waterford.	W.
1700.	,, William, Harperstown, Co. Wexford.	G.
1777.	**Horner,** Samuel, Finglas, Co. Dublin.	W.
1726.	**Hornsby,** Nathaniel, Dublin.	W.
1791.	**Hough,** Euphemia, widow, Wexford.	G.
1747.	**Houghton,** Anne, Dublin.	G.

IRISH WILLS: COPIES AND ABSTRACTS.

Date of Probate.			REFERENCE
1766.	**Houghton,** Charles, Mount Charles, Co. Wexford.		G.
1746.	,,	Edward, Dublin.	G.
1750.	,,	Edward, Dublin.	G.
1798.	,,	Edward, Dublin.	G.
1740.	,,	Elizabeth, widow Dublin.	G.
1729.	,,,	Henry, carver, Dublin.	G.
1751.	,,	Henry, Ross, Co. Wexford.	G.
1800.	,,	Henry, Balliane, Co. Wexford.	G.
1805.	,,	John, Dublin.	G.
1773.	,,	Joseph, merchant, Dublin.	G.
1765.	,,	Mary, alias **Grubb,** widow, New Ross.	G.
1748.	,,	Mathew, merchant, Dublin.	G.
1773.	,,	Captain Ralph, St. John's, Co. Wexford.	G.
1699.	,,	Rev. Robert, Vicar of Stabannan, Co. Louth.	G.
1702.	,,	Roger, Ballendesig, Co. Cork.	G.
1668.	,,	Thomas, merchant, Dublin.	G.
1741.	,,	Thomas, Kilmanock, Co. Wexford.	G.
1777.	**Houston,** Francis, Tullydowey, Co. Tyrone.		W.
1728.	,,	John, Castle Stewart, Co. Tyrone.	W.
1688.	**How,** Thomas, merchant, Dublin.		W.
1664.	**Howard,** Thomas, merchant, Dublin.		W.
1727.	,,	William, Dublin.	W.
1671.*	**Howes,** Robert, stationer, Dublin.		G.
1704.	**Howse,** Edward, Bandonbridge, Co. Cork.		G.
1727.	**Howth,** Thomas, Lord Baron of		W.
1718.	**Hubbart,** Nicholas, merchant, Cork.		G.
1770.	**Hubbert,** Elizabeth, widow, Cork.		G.
1670.	,,	Francis, Killeightroy, Co. Cork.	G.
1726.	**Hudspeth,** Thomas, sergeant in Col. Pocock's Regt.		W.
1739.	**Hughes,** Abraham.		G.
1765.	,,	Benjamin, Hilltown, Co. Wexford.	G.
1752.	,,	Elinor, widow, Enniscorthy.	G.
1795.	,,	Harry, Ballytrent, Co. Wexford.	G.
1800.	,,	Paul, Dublin.	G.
1818.	**Hume,** V. Rev. John, Dean of Derry.		H., · p.118

IRISH WILLS: COPIES AND ABSTRACTS.

Date of Probate.		REFERENCE.
1728.	**Hunt,** Edward, Dublin.	W.
1769.*	,, Robert, Inchirourke, Co. Limerick.	U.
1682.	**Huse,** Thomas, merchant, Dublin.	W.
1720.	**Huson,** Benjamin, clerk, Dromiskin, Co. Louth.	G.
1736.	,, Elizabeth, Tomnaboley.	G.
1809.	,, Richard, Dublin.	G.
1666.	**Hussey,** Bartholomew, Enniscorthy, Co. Wexford.	W.
1664.	,, Patrick, Baron of Galtrim, Co. Meath.	W.
1666.	,, Peter, Culmullen, Co. Meath.	W.
1728.	**Hutchinson,** Hugh, Bantry, Co. Cork.	W.
1729.	,, John, Ballyrea, Co. Armagh.	W.
1708.	**Hutton,** John, inn-holder, Dublin.	W.
1728.	**Hyde,** John, bookseller, Dublin.	W.
1468.	**Hygdon,** Agnes, alias **Duff.**	T. & B., p.6.
1777.	**Hyndman,** Archibald, merchant, Belfast, Co. Antrim.	W.
1674.	**Inchiquin,** Morogh, Earl of	G.
1777.	,, William, Earl of	W.
1727.	**Irvine,** Archibald, Drumchay, Co. Fermanagh.	W.
1778.*	**Irwin,** John, Drumsilla, Co. Leitrim.	M. Vol. XII, 461.
1777.	,, John, silkweaver, Park Street, Dublin.	W.
1680.	**Isaac,** Robert, mariner, Minehead, Somerset.	W.
1730.	**Jackson,** Beresford, Maghryenan.	G.
1707.	,, Rev. Daniel, clerk, Santry, Co. Dublin.	W.
1667.	,, Edmond, Curludy, Co. Kilkenny.	W.
1741.	,, Isabella, widow.	G.
1707.	,, William, Bray, Co. Wicklow.	W.
1756.	**Jacob,** John, Rathdowney, Co. Wexford.	G.
1668.	,, William, Sigginstown.	G.
1730.	**James,** Richard, Carnew.	G.
1728.	**Jameson,** John, Sligo.	W.
1667.	**Jean,** David, St. Andrew's Parish, Dublin.	W.
1823.	**Jenkins,** William, M.D., Bandon, Co. Cork.	G.
1679.	**Jennings,** Robert, Kilkea, Co. Kildare.	W.
1786.	**Jephson,** Anne, alias **Butler.**	G.

Date of Probate.			REFERENCE
1756.	**Jephson,** Anthony, Mallow, Co. Cork.		G.
1789.	,,	Deborah, widow, Mallow, Co. Cork.	G.
1781.*	,,	Denham, Mallow, Co. Cork.	G.
1788.	,,	Henry, Knockangriffin, Co. Cork.	G.
1638.	,,	Sir John, Kt., Froyle, Hants.	O. Lee, 133.
1698.	,,	John, Moyalla, Co. Cork.	G.
1724.	,,	John, Limerick.	G.
1766.	,,	John, Carrick-on-Suir, Co. Tipperary.	G.
1655.	,,	Dame Mary, widow.	G.
1698.	,,	Michael, Dean of St. Patrick's, Dublin.	G
1769.	,,	Rev. Norris, Mallow, Co. Cork.	G.
1771.	,,	Osborne, Carrick-on-Suir, Co. Tipperary.	G.
1803.	,,	Robert, Blackrock, Co. Dublin.	G.
1660.	,,	William, late of Froyle, Hants	G.
1720.	,,	William, Dean of Lismore.	G.
1779.	,,	William, Innishannon, Co. Cork.	G.
1778.	**Jessop,** Thomas, Mount Jessop, Co. Longford.		M. Vol. XI, 3?
1729.	**Jevers,** John, Dublin.		W.
1764.	**Jewell,** Abraham, Royal Hospital, Kilmainham.		G.
1658.	,,	Andrew, late of Athlone, Co. Westmeath.	G.
1706.	,,	Anne, widow, Ballinelard, Co. Tipperary.	G.
1705.	,,	William, Ballinelard, Co. Tipperary.	G.
1675.	**John,** Isaac, goldsmith, Dublin.		W.
1682.	**Johnson,** Christopher, Dublin.		W.
1728.	,,	Esther, spinster, Dublin.	W.
1727.	**Johnston,** Anne Jane, spinster.		W.
1675.	,,	David, merchant, Dublin.	W.
1777.	,,	Francis, Corkeran, Co. Monaghan.	W.
1676.	,,	James, Aghmuldony, Co. Fermanagh.	W.
1708.	,,	James, Glyn, Co. Antrim.	W.
1706.	,,	Richard, Emy, Co. Monaghan.	W.
1728.	,,	William, M.D., Warwick, Warwickshire.	W.
1777.	**Jolly,** David, cordwainer, Killinolog, King's Co.		W.
1810.	**Jones,** Abraham, Coolattin, Co. Wicklow.		G.
1707.	,,	Adam, butcher, Dublin.	W.

IRISH WILLS: COPIES AND ABSTRACTS.

Date of Probate.			REFERENCE.
1697.	**Jones,**	Ambrose, Cashel.	G.
1734.	,,	Ambrose, Drewstown, Co. Meath.	G.
1786.	,,	Ambrose, Jonesborough, Co. Meath.	G.
1777.	,,	Ann, widow, Newtown-Perry, Limerick.	W.
1716.	,,	Arthur, Dublin.	G.
1671.	,,	Bryan, Dublin.	N. Vol. 151, p.114.
1786.	,,	David, Beauparc, Co. Meath.	G.
1726.	,,	Edward, cork cutter, Dublin.	G.
1677.	,,	Elizabeth, widow of Dr. John Jones, Dublin.	W.
1822.*	,,	Emma Morris, Liscarrick, Co. Antrim.	G.
1673.	,,	Frances, spinster, Dublin.	G.
1813.	,,	Frederick Edward, Jonesborough, Co. Meath.	G.
1674.	,,	Henry, St. Nicholas-street, Dublin.	W.
1681.	,,	Henry, Bishop of Meath.	W.
1728.	,,	Hugh, freeholder, Ticknicke, Co. Dublin.	G.
1788.	,,	Isabella, widow, Tintern Abbey, Co. Wexford.	G.
1695.	,,	Joan, widow, alias **Howard,** Dublin.	G.
1686.	,,	John, Moyallow, Co. Cork.	G.
1760.	,,	John, mariner, Howth, Co. Dublin.	G.
1770.	,,	John, alderman, Limerick.	G.
1811.	,,	Margaret, spinster, Coolattin, Co. Wicklow.	G.
1664.	,,	Morris, Dublin.	G.
1695.	,,	Nicholas, Dublin.	G.
1664.	,,	Oliver, lieut.-colonel.	W.
1695.	,,	Oliver, 2nd justice, K.B.	G.
1688.*	,,	Owen, Dublin.	G.
1725.	,,	Rath, Dublin.	G.
1695.	,,	Richard, Dublin.	G.
1719.	,,	Robert, baker.	G.
1676.	,,	Roger, Laziehill, Dublin.	W.
1677.	,,	Roger, Dublin.	W.
1748.	,,	Roger, Dollardstown, Co. Meath	G.
1667.	,,	Thomas, brewer, Dublin.	G.
1676.	,,	Thomas, alderman, Dublin.	W.
1719.	,,	Thomas, brewer, Dublin.	G.

IRISH WILLS: COPIES AND ABSTRACTS.

Date of Probate.		REFERENCE
1738.	**Jones,** Thomas, Oldcastle, Co. Meath.	G.
1765.	,, Thomas, Nessington, Co. Meath.	G.
1777.	,, Thomas, ironmonger, Waterford.	W.
1813.*	,, Thomas Morris, Moneyglass, Co. Antrim.	G.
1693.	,, Valentine, Killmacmurearty, Co. Armagh.	G.
1761.	,, Valentine, Lisburn, Co. Antrim.	G
1687.	,, William, Castleconrath, Co. Westmeath.	G.
1696.	,, William, Dublin.	G.
1729.	,, William, merchant, Dublin.	W.
1735.	,, William Morris, Moneyglass, Co. Antrim.	G.
1859.	**Justice,** Henry Chinnery, barrister, Dublin.	G.
1767.	,, John, Ballynrudellig, Co. Kerry.	G.
1799.	,, Thomas, Ballysimon, Co. Kerry.	G.
1727.	**Kane,** Joseph, alderman, Dublin.	W.
1813.	,, Patrick, shopkeeper, Multifarnham, Co. Westmeath.	W.
1735.*	,, Richard, Carrickfergus.	G.
1747.	,, Thomas, vintner, Dublin.	G.
1679.	**Kavanagh,** Griffin, Boderene, Co. Wexford.	W.
1813.	,, Mary, spinster, Cork.	W.
1813.	,, Michael, sugar-baker, Dublin.	W.
1678.	**Kealy,** John, Gowran, Co. Kilkenny.	W.
1726.	**Kean,** Bartholomew.	W.
1769.	,, Mary, alias **Rorke,** Ballinamore, Co. Leitrim.	N. Vol. 149 p.26.
1729.	**Keanan,** James.	W.
1777.	**Keane,** Sarah, widow, Britain-Street, Dublin.	W.
1633.*	**Kearny,** Edmond, merchant, Killmallock.	W.
1777.	**Keating,** Maurice, Bath.	W.
1765.*	,, Nicholas, Dublin.	G.
1813.	,, Patrick, starch manufacturer, Dublin.	W.
1778.	,, Richard, glover, Cork.	G.
1813.	**Keatinge,** Thomas, Kells, Co. Meath.	G. & M., V XII, 458.
1679.	**Keatting,** John, Gurteen, Co. Waterford.	W.
1680.	,, Oliver, Ballynunnery, Co. Carlow.	W.
1813.	**Keeffe,** Daniel, Kinsale, Co. Cork.	W.

IRISH WILLS: COPIES AND ABSTRACTS.

Date of Probate.			REFERENCE.
1813.	**Keely,**	Mary, widow, Dublin.	W.
1680.	**Keigh,**	Laughlin, salt-boiler, Laziehill, Dublin.	W.
1728.	**Keith,**	Jeremiah, merchant, Coote-hill, Co. Cavan.	W.
1777.	**Kelburn,**	Ebenezer, clerk, Dublin.	W.
1813.	**Kellett,**	Helena, widow, Clonmell.	W.
1813.	**Kelly,**	Denis, Dublin.	W.
1813.	,,	Edward, Clonmore, Co. Wexford.	W.
1729.	,,	Francis, Mary's Lane, Dublin.	W.
1777.	,,	John, Lanesborough, Co. Longford.	W.
1745.*	,,	Laughlin, Lysmoyle, Co. Roscommon.	N. v. 149, p.25.
1777.	,,	Mary, Dublin.	W.
1777.	,,	Peter, merchant, Kildare St., Dublin.	W.
1813.	,,	Robert, Dundalkin, Co. Louth.	W.
1471.	,,	Thomas, Skiddoo.	T. & B., p.19.
1667.	**Kelson,**	John, Drumbony, Limerick City.	W.
1471.	**Kempe,**	John.	T. & B., p.14.
1676.	**Kempston,**	Nicholas, Drummurry, Co. Cavan.	W.
1474.	**Kenane,**	Patrick.	T. & B., p.82.
1777.	**Kendall,**	James, Dublin.	W.
1777.	**Kennan,**	Jane, widow, Dublin.	W.
1729.	**Kennedy,**	Barthsheba, widow, Dublin.	W.
1813.	,,	Charles, Thornhill, Co. Down.	W.
1685.	,,	David, Ballycultra, Co. Down.	G.
1792.	,,	Esther, widow, Londonderry.	G.
1727.	,,	Henry, Graguenafin, King's Co.	W.
1695.	,,	Hugh, Derfraghrog, Co. Tyrone.	G.
1760.	,,	Hugh.	G.
1662.	,,	James, clerk, Donegal.	G.
1681.	,,	John, Bellimegown.	G.
1813.	,,	Samuel, haberdasher, Dublin.	W.
1726.	,,	William, Yeoman of the Guards, Dublin.	W.
1744.	,,	William, Mullo, Co. Longford.	G.
1783.	,,	William, Londonderry.	G.
1708.	**Kenney,**	Thomas, capt. H.M.S. Falmouth.	W.
1682.	**Kenny,**	Richard, Wexford.	W.

IRISH WILLS: COPIES AND ABSTRACTS.

Date of Probate.			REFERENCE.
1664.	**Kent,** Thomas, Danestown, Co. Meath.		W.
1818.	**Keny,** Elizabeth.		W.
1793.	**Keon,** Ann, Dublin.		N. v. 149, p.363.
1744.*	,,	Bridget, widow, Brendrum, Co. Leitrim.	N. v. 149, p.363.
1744.*	,,	Myles, Brendrum, Co. Leitrim.	N. v. 149, p.363.
1811.	,,	Myles, Keonbrook, Co. Leitrim.	N. v. 149, p.364.
1794.	,,	Robert, Dublin.	N. v. 149, p.364.
1801.	,,	William, Dublin.	N. v. 149, p.364.
1777.	**Keough,** Michael, Athlone, Co. Roscommon.		W.
1818.	**Kerby,** Samuel, Drumkeen.		W.
1676.*	**Kerdiffe,** William, Kerdiffestown, Co. Kildare.		W.
1813.	**Kerin,** Terence, farmer, Scahane, Co. Clare.		W.
1679.	**Kerr,** Robert, Ballyaghrane, Co. Londonderry.		W.
1665.	**Kett,** John, merchant, Dublin.		W.
1474.	**Ketyng,** Nicholas, Clondalkin, Co. Dublin.		T. & B., p.112.
1675.	**Kieran,** John, brewer, New-row, Thomas-Court.		W.
1679.	**Kildare,** Ambrose Jones, Bishop of.		W.
1666.	,,	Elizabeth, Countess of.	W.
1665.	**King,** Francis, Radoony, Co. Sligo.		W.
1727.	,,	James, merchant, Dublin.	W
1728.	,,	John, brewer, Co. Dublin.	W.
1666.	,,	Ralph, recorder of Derry.	W.
1636.	,,	Richard, Kenéigh, Co. Cork.	G.
1708.	,,	Sir Robert, Bart., Rockingham, Co. Roscommon.	W.
1706.	,,	Sir William, Kt., Kilpeacon, Co. Limerick.	W.
1727.	**Kingsland,** Nicholas, Lord Viscount.		W.
1676.	**Kingston,** Lord John.		W.
1707.	**Kinkead,** William, linen-draper, Aughastrike, Co. Down.		W.
1719.*	**Kirby,** Nicholas, Callasin, Co. Cork.		G.
1729.	**Kirkwood,** Andrew, Killala, Co. Mayo.		W.
1813.	**Kirwan,** or **Kirwin,** Andrew, Galway.		W.
1777.	,,	Annabelle, widow, Galway.	W.
1676.	**Kirwood,** William, silk-man, All Hallows, Lombard-Street.		W.
1777.	**Kittson,** William, Ballyng, Co. Kilkenny.		W.
1728.	**Knight,** Christopher, Ballynoe, Co. Cork.		W.

IRISH WILLS: COPIES AND ABSTRACTS.

Date of Probate.		REFERENCE.
1726.	**Knight,** James, Dublin.	W.
1777.	,, Richard, Knightsgrove, Co. Longford.	W.
1818.	**Knipe,** John, Strandville, Co. Dublin.	W.
1666.	**Kniveton,** Henry, Dublin.	W.
1667.	**Knott,** John, clothier, Dublin.	W.
1818.	**Knox,** Francis, Rappa Castle, Co. Mayo.	W.
1681.	,, George, Morimore, Co. Donegal.	W.
1818.	,, Robert, Waterford.	W.
1728.	,, Thomas, Dungannon, Co. Tyrone.	W.
1706.	,, William, Castlereagh, Co. Mayo.	W.
1588.*	**Kyfte,** Nicholas, Portugal.	G.
1478.	**Kymore,** Ellen.	T. & B., p.103.
1726.	**La Baslme,** Gaspard.	W.
1773.	**Lacey,** James, hosier, Dublin.	N. v. 149, p.24.
1707.	**Lackey,** Robert, farmer, Ballykealy, Co. Carlow.	W.
1785.	**Lacy,** Andrew, clothier, Crooked Staff, Dublin.	N. v. 149, p.24.
1755.	,, Matthew.	N. v. 149, p.24.
1721.	,, Thomas, farmer, Jordanstown, Co. Meath.	N. v. 149, p.24.
1756.	,, William, Lisurelin, Co. Limerick.	N. v. 149, p.24.
1675.	**Ladd,** Henry, Dublin.	W.
1665.	**Ladyman,** Richard, linen-draper, Dublin.	W.
1688.*	,, Samuel, Archdeacon of Limerick.	A. Vol. 1858-9, p.117.
1777.	**Laffan,** Thomas, Kilkenny.	W.
1729.	**Lafite,** Matthew, Dublin.	W.
1818.	**Lahy,** Thomas, Williamstown, Co. Westmeath.	W.
1729.	**Lalor,** Elizabeth, Dublin.	W.
1728.	,, John, farmer, Munny, Queen's Co.	W.
1818.	**Lambert,** Joseph, Brookhill, Co. Mayo.	W.
1729.	**Lancaster,** Charles, Hawkhurst, Kent.	W.
1706.	**Lane,** Francis, capt. in Langston's Regt. of Horse.	W.
1728.*	,, Gawen, merchant, Cork.	G.
1662.	,, Richard, Cork.	G
1667.	,, Sampson.	W.
1700.	,, Thomas, Dromagh, Co. Cork.	G.

IRISH WILLS: COPIES AND ABSTRACTS.

Date of Probate.		Reference
1720.	**Lane,** Walter, Cork.	G.
1777.	,, William, Drogheda.	W.
1683.	**Lanesborough,** George, Lord Viscount.	W.
1683.	**Lang,** John, Ballygillgane, Co. Sligo.	W.
1473.	**Langan,** Cecily.	T. & B., p.65.
1813.	,, James, farmer, Greenogue, Co. Meath.	W.
1768.	**Langford,** Elizabeth, widow, Kells, Co. Limerick.	G.
1734.	,, Gertrude, widow, Doneraile, Co. Cork.	G.
1683.	,, Sir Hercules, Bart., Summerhill, Co. Meath.	W.
1755.	,, John, Kells, Co. Limerick.	G
1738.	,, Robert, Banemore, Co. Limerick.	G.
1726.	,, Susanna, spinster, St. Paul's, Covent Garden, London.	G.
1718.	,, Theophilus, Kinsale, Co. Cork.	G.
1650.	,, William, Cork.	G.
1719.	,, William, Gardenfield, Co. Limerick.	G.
1708.	**Langham,** Anne, widow, Dublin.	W.
1813.	**Langson,** John, gunmaker, Dublin.	W.
1813.	**Lannon,** John, Clare, Co. Mayo.	W.
1476.	**Lanysdall,** Robert.	T. & B., p.187
1721.	**Lapp,** Mary, widow, Cork.	G.
1691.	,, Richard, Archdeacon of Cork.	G.
1706.	,, Thomas, tanner, Cork.	G.
1721.	,, William, Bandon, Co. Cork.	G.
1727.	**La Rimbliere,** James, Dublin.	W.
1665.	**Latimer,** Hugh, Pagestown, Co. Meath.	W.
1467.	**Laules,** William, Garristown, Co. Dublin.	T. & B., p.8.
1666.	**Lavallen,** Patrick, alderman, Cork.	W.
1681.	**Lavallin,** James, Waterstown, Co. Cork.	W.
1728.	**Lavit,** Joseph, merchant, Cork.	W.
1476.	**Laweles,** Agnes, alias **Fox.**	T. & B., p.184
1474.	,, Patrick, Tallaght.	T. & B., p.145
1726.	**Lawles,** Mary, alias **Burke,** widow, Kilkenny.	W.
1707.	**Lawrence,** James, mariner, Lazyhill, Dublin.	W.
1703.	**Lawton,** Abraham, Mallow, Co. Cork.	G.
1758.*	,, Freyer, merchant, Cork.	G.

IRISH WILLS: COPIES AND ABSTRACTS.

Date of Probate.		REFERENCE.
1726.	**Lawton,** Hugh, farmer, Ballybeg, Co. Cork.	W. & G
1773.	,, John, Cork.	G.
1677.	**Layng,** John, clerk, Killashandra, Co. Cavan.	W.
1727.	**Leadbeater,** William, cardmaker, Dublin.	W.
1768.	**Leader,** Edward, Mount Leader, Co. Cork.	G.
1771.	,, Henry, Tullig, Co. Cork.	G.
1766.	,, John, Keal, Co. Cork.	G.
1727.	**Leake,** Ezekiel, Holycross, Tipperary.	W.
1727.	,, Pierce, Newcastle, Co. Limerick.	W.
1813.	**Leathem,** Samuel, Londonderry.	W.
1738.	**Leathes,** Margaret, Hillsborough, Co. Down.	G.
1788.	**Ledbetter,** Joseph, Bandon, Co. Cork.	G.
1793.	,, Joseph, Bandon, Co. Cork.	G.
1800.	**Ledsam,** John, grocer, Dublin.	G.
1806.	,, John, Dublin.	G.
1805.	,, Sarah, widow, Dublin.	G.
1797.	**Ledwick,** Susannah, widow, Dublin.	H., p.110.
1804.*	,, Rev. William,	H., p.112.
1676.	**Ledwicke,** Pierce, Portelare, Co. Roscommon.	W.
1726.	**Lee,** Edward, Barnarusacully, Co. Tipperary.	W.
1813.	,, George, Barna, Co. Tipperary.	W.
1708.	,, Richard, Clanderlaw, Co. Clare.	W.
1813.	**Le Grand,** Rev. Gilbert Oliver, priest, Dublin.	W.
1706.	**Leigh,** Andrew, Friarstown, Co. Kildare.	W.
1727.	,, Francis Robert, Dublin.	W.
1729.	,, James, Waterstown, Co. Louth.	W.
1727.	,, Rev. Thomas, rector of Haynestown, Co. Louth.	W.
1708.	**Le Large,** Robert, merchant, Dublin.	W.
1675.	**Lenox,** William, the elder, Woohead, Co. Derry.	W.
1813.	**Lentaigne,** Benjamin, Dublin.	W.
1777.	**Leonard,** John, Brownstown, Co. Kildare.	W.
1727.	**Lesac,** Peter, merchant, Dublin.	W.
1777.	**L'Estrange,** Edmund, Keoltown.	W.
1666.	,, Henry, Moystown, King's Co.	W.
1677.	,, William, Castle Cuffe, Queen's Co.	W.

IRISH WILLS: COPIES AND ABSTRACTS.

Date of Probate.		REFERENCE.
1727.	**Lewis,** Thomas, senior, Aughmacart, Queens Co.	W.
1678.	**Lewys,** Sir John, Bart., London.	W.
1757.	**Leyn,** Christopher, Killballyporter, Co. Meath.	N. v. 149, p.2ł
1758.	,, Christopher, Killballyporter, Co. Meath.	N. v. 149, p.2ł
1706.	**Leynes,** Alson, widow, alias **Hore,** Dublin.	W.
1706.	**Lifsley,** James, merchant, Dublin.	W.
1677.	**Lincorne,** Catherine, alias **Tancard,** widow, Dublin.	W.
1683.	**Lindsay,** Fergus, tanner, Ballyma' Richard, Co. Antrim.	W.
1813.	,, James, tanner, Waterside, Londonderry.	W.
1708.	**Linegar,** John, Dunbroe, Co. Dublin.	W.
1677.	**Littell,** Francis, Dublin.	W.
1726.	**Little,** John, Lisnanaugh, Co. Longford.	W.
1813.	,, Joseph, Presbyterian minister, Killeleagh, Co. Down.	W.
1665.	**Lloyd,** Owen, Abbeyboyle, Co. Roscommon.	W.
1672.*	**Lochard,** Peter, Pimlico, Dublin.	G.
1734.	**Lockhart,** Arthur, Christianstown, Co. Kildare.	G.
1679.	**Loftus,** Adam, archbishop of Dublin.	M. vol. XI, 36ł
1666.	,, Sir Arthur, Kt., Dublin.	W.
1707.	,, Henry, Loftus Hall, Co. Wexford.	W.
1659.*	,, Robert, Co. Dublin.	W.
1728.	**Logan,** Jane, Parish St. Clement Danes, Middlesex.	W.
1729.	**Loghlin,** Michael, Carrick, Co. Tipperary.	W.
1474.	**Lok,** Nicholas.	T. & B., p.11ł
1813.	**Lombard,** Catherine, widow, Killarney.	W.
1648.	,, Edmond, Cork.	G.
1749.	,, George, merchant, Cork.	G.
1769.	,, George, merchant, Cork.	G.
1639.	,, James, merchant, Cork.	G.
1652.	,, James, alderman, Cork.	G.
1783.	,, James, merchant, Cork.	G.
1764.	,, John, Gortmalyre, Co. Cork.	G.
1769.	,, Jones, Cork.	G.
1626.	,, Nicholas, Cork.	G.
1718.	,, William, Cork.	G.
1754.	,, William, merchant, Cork	G.

IRISH WILLS: COPIES AND ABSTRACTS.

Date of Probate.		REFERENCE.
1818.	**Long,** Thomas, Inistioge, Co. Kilkenny.	W.
1740.	**Longfield,** Hawnby, Ballynascarty, Co. Cork.	G.
1730.	,, John, Castle Mary, Co. Cork.	G.
1765.	,, John, Longueville, Co. Cork.	G.
1751.	,, Mary, widow, Kilmacow, Co. Cork.	G.
1765.	,, Robert, Castle Mary, Co. Cork.	G.
1666.	**Longford,** Henry, Enniskillen, Co. Fermanagh.	W.
1777.	**Longworth,** Elizabeth, widow, Dublin.	W.
1686.	**Looby,** Baptist, cordwainer, Cork.	G.
1714.	,, George, brewer, Cork.	G.
1728.	**Lord,** Edward, apothecary, Dublin.	W.
1777.	,, William, Dunleary, Co. Dublin.	W.
1727.	**Lostau,** Bernard, Colonel Hawley's Regiment of Foot.	W.
1728.	**Love,** Joseph, Dublin.	W.
1818.	,, William, Cork.	W.
1707.	**Lovell,** Rev. George, Tullymore, Co. Antrim.	W.
1706.	,, Jane, widow, London.	W.
1777.	**Lovett,** Clotilda.	G. & W.
1777.	**Low,** Eusebius, Dublin.	W.
1624.	**Lowther,** Sir Gerard, Kt., Jus. Common Pleas.	L.
1660.	,, Sir Gerald, Kt., Jus. Common Pleas.	L.
1727.	**Lucas,** Benjamin, Ballingaddy, Co. Clare.	W.
1664.	,, Edward, Dublin.	W.
1818.	,, Samuel, Springfield, King's Co.	W.
1727.	,, Thomas, Castle Shane, Co. Monaghan.	W.
1724.	**Ludlow,** Stephen, Dublin.	G.
1686.	**Luffkin,** Grizzel, Farrenebane, Co. Cork.	G.
1710.	,, John, Raheen, Co. Cork.	G.
1724.	,, Roger, Knocknahilan, Co. Cork.	G.
1708.	**Lumm,** Elnathan, banker, Dublin.	W.
1702.	**Luther,** Elizabeth, widow, Youghal, Co. Cork.	G.
1676.	**Luttrell,** William, School-House Lane, Dublin.	W.
1677.	**Lynagerr,** John, Dublin.	W.
1818.	**Lynass,** Kennedy, Dublin.	W.
1781.*	**Lynch,** Edward, Rathorpe, Co. Galway.	G.

IRISH WILLS: COPIES AND ABSTRACTS.

Date of Probate.		REFERENCE.
1777.	**Lynch,** Henry, Clogher, Co. Mayo.	W.
1726.	,, Mary, spinster, Dublin.	W.
1777.	,, Mary, widow, Galway.	W.
1813.	,, Mary Elizabeth, spinster, Cork.	W.
1813.	,, Michael Henry, Allsops buildings, Middlesex.	W.
1675.	,, Nicholas, Craigmoor, Co. Galway.	W.
1728.	,, William, Keilticona, King's Co.	W.
1727.	**Lyndon,** Edward, Dublin.	W.
1698.*	,, Jane, Carrickfergus.	G.
1699.	,, Sir John, Kt.	G.
1775.	**Lyon,** Cornelius, Rathnee, Co. Cork.	G.
1751.	,, John, Cork.	G.
1777.	,, John, alderman, Waterford.	W.
1780.	,, Robert, shopkeeper, Cork.	G.
1772.	,, Timothy, gardener, Cork.	G.
1777.	**Lyons,** Denis, farmer, Croom, Co. Limerick.	W.
1739.	**McAboy,** David, Knockasmullane, Co. Cork.	G.
1729.	**McAdam,** Philip, Gortalogher, Co. Clare.	W.
1813.	**McArdle,** Mary, widow, Dublin.	W.
1813.	**McAuley,** or **McGawley,** Peter.	W.
1813.	**McBurney,** John, farmer, Corrag, Co. Down.	W.
1715.	**McCarthy,** Callaghan, Cahircreveen, Co. Cork.	G.
1725.*	,, Charles, Droumagarry, Co. Cork.	G.
1727.	,, Charles, Ballyshoneen, Co. Cork.	G.
1728.	,, Charles, merchant, Dublin.	W.
1656.*	,, Cormack McDonough, Duhallow, Co. Cork.	G.
1732.	,, Donough, Derry, Co. Cork.	G.
1813.	,, Michael, Dublin.	W.
1728.	**McCausland,** John, Strabane, Co. Tyrone.	W.
1722.	,, Oliver, Strabane, Co. Tyrone.	G.
1741.	,, Oliver, Strabane, Co. Tyrone.	G.
1813.	,, Oliver, Bristol.	W.
1813.	**McClaughry,** Mary Ann, widow, Kilkenny.	W.
1813.	**McClelland,** John, Philipstown, King's Co.	W.
1813.	**McClenechan,** Charles, Dublin and Chelsea.	W.

IRISH WILLS: COPIES AND ABSTRACTS.

Date of Probate.		Reference.
1707.	**McClintock,** John, Trentogh, Co. Donegal.	W.
1728.	**McCraith,** John, farmer, Hammamtown, Co. Limerick.	W.
1728.	**McCulloch,** Henry, Fewghoge, Co. Antrim.	W.
1682.	,, William, Raneldstown, Co. Antrim.	W.
1728.	**McDaniel,** Mary, widow, Coombe, Dublin.	W.
1813.	**McDermott,** Uyles, Belturbet, Co. Cavan.	W.
1728.	**McDermottroe,** Bryan, Castletehyn, Co. Roscommon.	W
1728.	**McDonnell,** Dame Hannah, widow.	W.
1813.	**McDonogh,** William, Cooloughbane, Co. Mayo.	W.
1728.	**McDowell,** Benjamin, linen-draper, Rathmore, Co. Antrim.	W.
1808.	**McEvoy,** Francis, surgeon, Dublin.	N. v. 151, p.114.
1813.	,, Patrick, Dublin.	W.
1727.	**McGhee,** Theobald, Port M'Ghee, Co. Kerry.	W.
1683.	**McGill,** James, Ballymonestragh, Co. Down.	W.
1755.	**McGines,** James, merchant, Dizart, Co. Louth.	G.
1804.	**McGiness,** John, Upper Brockagh.	G.
1736.	**McGinis,** Con, farmer, Drumbenagh, Co. Monaghan.	G.
1767.	**McGinness,** Owen, Galway.	G.
1777.	**McGinniss,** Honora, widow, Galway.	G.
1727.	**McGuire,** Richard, banker, Dublin.	G.
1700.	**McGwyre,** Bryan, Carrick, Co. Tipperary.	G.
1813.	**McKenna,** Mary, widow, Stackallen.	W.
1741.	**McKeone,** Anthony, Gt. Johnstown, Co. Longford.	N. v. 149, p.292.
1727.	**McLorinan,** Hugh, Anaghmore, Co. Antrim.	G.
1697.	,, Margaret, widow, Aghadremderege, Co. Tyrone.	G.
1744.	,, Matthew, Killcross, Co. Antrim.	G.
1750.	,, Michael, Randalstown, Co. Antrim.	G.
1665.	**McMahon,** Michael, merchant, Limerick.	W.
1813.	,, Terence, Dublin.	W.
1726.	**McManus,** James, Maynooth, Co. Kildare.	W.
1722.	,, Mary, alias **Dobbin,** widow, Carradonaghy, Co. Antrim.	G.
1813.	**McMillan,** John.	W.
1728.	**McNeal,** Archibald, Chancellor of Down Cathedral.	W.
1813.	**McNeelance,** John, Milltown, Co. Tyrone.	W.
1813.	**McNeill,** Charles, Castlederg, Co. Tyrone.	W.

IRISH WILLS: COPIES AND ABSTRACTS.

Date of Probate.		REFERENCE.
1708.	**McNemara,** John, merchant, Limerick.	W.
1788.	**McSweeny,** John, shoemaker, Cork.	G.
1782.	**McVittie,** William, Aghalisabea, Co. Monaghan.	G.
1818.	**Macale,** James, Corendoo, Galway.	W.
1818.	**Macan,** Turner, Green Mount Lodge, Co. Louth.	W.
1728.	**Macartney,** John, merchant, Belfast.	W.
1818.	**Macdonough,** Cornelius, Dublin.	W.
1818.	**Madden,** William, paper manufacturer, Dublin.	W.
1726.	**Madocks,** Samuel, merchant, Dublin.	W.
1727.	**Magaw,** John, clothier, Dublin.	W.
1729.	**Magawley,** John, Tully, Co. Westmeath.	W.
1818.	**Magee,** Bryan, Ballynagerick, Co. Down.	W.
1763.	,, Nicholas, Lisburn, Co. Antrim.	G.
1629.	**Magenis,** Arthur ,Lord Viscount of Ivoagh, Rathfriland, Co. Down.	''
1735.	,, Arthur, Cabragh, Co. Down.	G.
1790.	,, Arthur, Ballsgrove, Drogheda.	G.
1755.	,, Con, Newry.	G.
1664.	,, Constantine, Dublin.	G
1726.	,, Daniel, Castlewellan, Co. Down.	G.
1758.*	,, Daniel, Sanrod, Co. Down.	G.
1808.	,, Colonel Hugh, Dublin.	G.
1803.	,, John, Dublin.	G.
1804.	,, John, Dublin.	G.
1747.	,, Mary.	G.
1765.	,, Mary, widow, Lurgan, Co. Down.	G.
1706.	,, Phelemy, Castlewellan, Co. Down.	G.
1807.	,, Richard, Waringstown, Co. Down.	G.
1756.	**Magennis,** Arthur.	G.
1807.	,, Edward, linen draper, Lisburn, Co. Antrim.	G.
1751.	,, Thomas, Naventown, Co. Meath.	G.
1748.	**Maginnis,** Edmund, Londonderry.	G.
1789.	,, Hugh, Magerlane, Co. Antrim.	G.
1799.	**Maginniss,** Hamilton, Londonderry.	G.
1831.	,, Sir John, Kt., Londonderry.	G.
1818.	**Magner,** James, corn merchant, Cork.	W.

IRISH WILLS: COPIES AND ABSTRACTS.

Date of Probate.		REFERENCE.
1640.	**Magnise,** Hugh, Newry, Co. Down.	G.
1813.	**Maguire,** Francis, Greaghnafind, Co. Fermanagh.	W.
1727.	**Mahon,** Charles, linen draper, Back-lane, Dublin.	W.
1813.	,, Rev. Maurice, Dublin.	W.
1726.	**Mainaduc,** Alcide Bonniot, refugee, Cork City.	W.
1813.	**Manders,** Isaac, Rathmines, Co. Dublin.	W.
1813.	,, Joshua, Dublin.	W.
1726.	**Mangan,** Ellinor, alias **Litchfield,** widow, Legacurrin, Queen's Co.	W.
1813.	**Mansergh,** James, Limerick.	W.
1707.	,, William, St. Clement Danes, Middlesex.	W.
1727.	**Manwaring,** William, Maynooth, Co. Kildare.	W.
1669.	**Manwood,** Col. Jerome, Woolwich, Kent.	W.
1813.	**Mara,** Dennis.	W.
1784.	**Marlay,** Thomas, Celbridge, Co. Kildare.	M. vol. XII, p.365.
1728.	**Marple,** or **Marples,** Richard, Meath St., Dublin.	W.
1813.	**Marshall,** Celia, widow, Dublin.	W.
1776.	**Martin,** Alexander, Bandon, Co. Cork.	G.
1667.	,, Catharine, widow of John Martin.	W.
1666.	,, Edward, alderman, Drogheda.	W.
1727.	,, Henry, Knockingin, Co. Dublin.	W.
1727.	,, James, merchant, Dublin.	W.
1813.	,, Patrick, brewer, Dundalk, Co. Louth.	W.
1813.	**Martley,** James Frederick, M.D., Kells.	W.
1729.	,, John, Ballyfallen, Co. Meath.	G.
1797.	,, John, Athboy.	G.
1707.	**Maslin,** William, innkeeper, Lisburn, Co. Antrim.	W.
1639.*	**Mason,** Robert, M.A., Eniskeene.	Y. Bundle, July, 1641-2.
1728.	,, Robert, Dublin.	W.
1813.	,, William, Derrylahane, Co. Tipperary.	W.
1665.	**Massereene,** John, Viscount.	W.
1813.	**Massey,** Charles, Tipperary.	W.
1693.	**Massie,** Samuel, merchant, Dublin.	G.
1813.	**Massy,** Hugh, Lord Baron, Dunbryleage, Co. Limerick.	W.
1726.	**Masterson,** Elinor, alias **York,** Dublin.	W.

IRISH WILLS: COPIES AND ABSTRACTS.

Date of Probate.		REFERENCE.
1729.	**Mathers,** Thomas, clerk, Ballynaghy, Co. Armagh.	W.
1667.	**Mathew,** John, clerk, Dublin.	W.
1664.	**Maw,** Robert, cutler, Dublin.	W.
1684.	**Maxwell,** Agnes, Drumbeg, Co. Down.	G.
1720.*	,, Arthur, Drumbeg, Co. Down.	G.
1729.	,, Hugh, Rooban, Co. Down.	W.
1682.	,, James, Drumbeg, Co. Down.	G.
1772.	,, James, the elder, Omagh, Co. Tyrone.	G.
1717.	,, John.	G.
1709.*	,, Mary, Strabane, Co. Tyrone.	G.
1813.	,, Rainy, Belfast.	W.
1779.*	,, Robert, Killyfadey, Co. Derry.	G
1702.*	,, Thomas, Strabane, Co. Tyrone.	G.
1709.	,, William, merchant, Strabane, Co. Tyrone.	G.
1666.	**Maynwaringe,** Dudley, Dublin.	W.
1791.	**Meacham,** William, lieut. in 28th Regt. of Foot.	G.
1707.	**Mead,** Sir John, Bart., Ballintober, Co. Cork.	W.
1728.	**Meade,** Andrew, Newcastle, Co. Limerick.	W.
1747.*	,, John, Ballykeale, Co. Kildare.	N. v. 151, p.118
1729.	**Meagher,** Nicholas, shoemaker, Golden-Bridge, Co. Tipperary.	W.
1813.	**Meares,** Mary, widow, Mearescourt, Co. Westmeath.	W.
1729.	**Medcalfe,** Thomas, cordwainer, Dublin.	W.
1729.	**Medlicott,** Elizabeth, Tully, Co. Kildare.	W.
1656.*	**Mee,** William, Kilrush, Co. Westmeath.	G.
1706.	**Mercier,** Claud, Fiddown, Co. Kilkenny.	W.
1729.	**Meredith,** Jane, widow, Cumber, Co. Down.	W.
1729.	,, Thomas, confectioner, Dublin.	W.
1726.	**Merefield,** Ellinor, spinster, Dublin.	W.
1707.	**Merrony,** Margaret, alias **Creagh,** widow.	W.
1699.	**Mertell,** Patrick, merchant, Cork.	G.
1653.	,, William, burgess, Cork.	G.
1758.	**Mertin,** Alexander, cordwainer.	G
1624.	,, John, yeoman, Bandonbridge, Co. Cork.	G.
1642.	,, John, Cork.	G.
1707.	**Meyler,** Nicholas, Dublin.	W.

IRISH WILLS: COPIES AND ABSTRACTS.

Date of Probate.			REFERENCE.
1729.	**Middleton,** James, Lanesborough, Co. Longford.		W.
1728.	**Midleton,** Alan, Lord Viscount.		W. & G.
1747.	,,	Anne, Dowager Lady Viscountess.	G.
1765.	,,	George, Lord Viscount.	G.
1747.	,,	Lord.	G.
1664.	**Miechelburn,** Abraham, Kilcranda, Co. Wicklow.		W.
1727.	**Mildmay,** Daniel, merchant, Antrim.		W.
1726.	**Miller,** James, Milford, Co. Mayo.		W.
1661.	,,	John, merchant, Dublin and Bristol.	G.
1658.	,,	Joseph, Rossgarland, Co. Wexford.	G.
1729.	,,	Joseph, clerk, Blackmore, Co. Wexford.	G.
1791.	,,	Joseph, clerk, Wexford.	G.
1704.*	,,	Lewis, Drinagh, Co. Wexford.	G.
1650.	,,	Ralph.	G.
1726.	,,	Robert, Milford, Co. Mayo.	W.
1687.	,,	Thomas, alderman, Limerick.	G.
1653.	,,	Captain William.	G.
1696.	,,	William, Morris Castle, Wexford.	G.
1691.	**Millerd,** Thomas, maltster, Cork.		G.
1813.	**Mills,** Mary, Dublin.		W.
1787.	,,	Samuel, Turnings, Co. Kildare.	G.
1813.	,,	Samuel Leonard, Hudson's Bay, Co. Roscommon.	W.
1819.	,,	Samuel, Co. Kildare.	G.
1699.	,,	Thomas, Ballybeg, Co. Cork.	G.
1720.	,,	Thomas, clerk, Ballymodan, Co. Cork.	G.
1737.	,,	Thomas, Cork.	G.
1813.	**Minchin,** Anna, spinster, Dublin.		W.
1681.	,,	Charles, Moneygall, King's Co.	W.
1682.	,,	John, baker, London.	W.
1841.	**Minhear,** William, merchant, Raleigh, Co. Cork.		G.
1755.	**Mitchell,** John, Mitchellsfort, Co. Cork.		G.
1758.	,,	Martha, widow, Cork.	G.
1711.	,,	Thomas, merchant, Cork.	G.
1721.	,,	Thomas, Aghada, Co. Cork.	G.
1752.	,,	Thomas, apothecary, Cork.	G.

IRISH WILLS: COPIES AND ABSTRACTS.

Date of Probate.		REFERENCE.
1813.	**Mitchell,** William, Monaghan.	W.
1632.*	**Moderwell,** Adam, the elder, Donaghmore, Co. Donegal.	G.
1697.	,, John, merchant, Strabane.	G
1813.	**Moilse,** James, Erno, Queen's Co.	W.
1474.	**Mold,** John.	T. & B., p.84.
1726.	**Molesworth,** John, Lord Viscount.	W.
1726.	**Mollineaux,** John, draper, London.	W.
1726.	**Monk,** or **Monck,** George, Dublin.	W.
1813.	**Monks,** Daniel, Dublin.	W.
1813.	**Montgomery,** George William, Dublin.	W.
1683.	,, William Barlisberry, Co. Dublin.	W.
1726.	**Moody,** Robert, gardener, Dublin.	W.
1729.	**Moor,** Ann, alias **Archer,** widow, Kilkenny.	W.
1726.	,, Trevor, Parsonstown, King's Co.	W.
1726.	**Moore,** Brabazon, Mount Ferrable, Co. Monaghan.	W.
1727.	,, Ellen, widow, Tullamore, King's Co.	W.
1813.	,, Ellenor, widow, Dublin.	W.
1762.	,, Henry William, Drumbanagher, Co. Armagh.	M. v. XII, 35'
1787.	,, Henry, Ballyaglish, Co. Limerick.	M. v. XII, 36:
1728.	,, Ignatius, Ballintry, Co. Meath.	W.
1728.	,, James, Ballenacreemor, Ballymoney.	W.
1671.	,, John, merchant, Dublin.	W.
1746.	,, Randall, Mounterrible, Co. Monaghan.	M. v. XII, 16(
1813.	,, Rebecca.	W.
1775.	,, Robert, Ardmayle, Co. Tipperary.	M. v. XII, 85(
1735.	,, William, Atherdee, Co. Louth.	M. v. XII, 16(
1803.	,, William, Tullyvin, Co. Cavan.	P.
1813.	**Moran,** William, smith and farmer, Damelstown, Co. Meath.	W.
1707.	**More,** John, merchant, Dublin.	W.
1729.	**Morgan,** Elizabeth, spinster, Dublin.	W.
1681.	,, Robert, Castletown, Co. Sligo.	W.
1726.	**Morley,** Martin, Clonfad, Co. Westmeath.	W.
1728.	**Morphy,** Jane, widow, Dublin.	W.
1678.	,, John, Swords, Co. Dublin.	W.
1729.	**Morres,** Andrew, Dublin.	W.

IRISH WILLS: COPIES AND ABSTRACTS.

Date of Probate.			Reference
1717.	**Morris,**	Edward, Old Court, Co. Dublin.	G.
1718.	,,	Edward, Mullagha, Co. Meath.	G.
1727.	,,	James, Castlemartin, Co. Kildare.	W.
1813.	,,	James, farmer, Moneyrick, Co. Antrim.	G.
1730.	,,	Jane, widow, Dublin.	G.
1708.	,,	Rev. John, Ballymully, Co. Tyrone.	W. & G.
1741.	,,	John, mariner, man-o-war, "Ripon."	G.
1753.*	,,	John, Drumrecomond, Co. Antrim.	G.
1735.	,,	Patrick, Silverwood, Co. Armagh.	G.
1783.	,,	Roger, Ardstraw, Co. Tyrone.	G
1694.	,,	Samuel, Ballybegan, Co. Kerry.	G.
1758.	,,	Samuel, Drum, Co. Monaghan.	G.
1804.	,,	Rev. Samuel, Glebe House, Co. Tyrone.	G.
1806.	,,	Solomon, Gortin, Co. Tyrone.	G.
1797.*	,,	Thomas, Lisburn, Co. Antrim.	G.
1813.	,,	Thomas, woollen-draper, Largan, Co. Armagh.	W.
1724.	,,	William, barrister-at-law, Dublin.	G.
1737.	**Morrison,**	William, Midleton, Co. Cork.	G.
1799.	**Mortimer,**	Rev. Robert.	G.
1728.	**Motley,**	Charles, Moon, Co. Kildare.	W.
1728.	,,	Edward, rector of Desartmartin.	W.
1728.	**Mullane,**	James, merchant, Cork.	G.
1729.	**Mulys,**	John, merchant, Dublin.	W.
1727.	**Murdock,**	Robert, merchant, Newry, Co. Down.	W.
1813.	**Murphy,**	Arthur, farmer, Donard, Co. Wicklow.	W.
1682.	,,	Martin, merchant, Athlone.	W.
1727.	,,	Richard, yeoman, Kilmacurra, Co. Wicklow.	W.
1664.	**Murry,**	John, Harbourstown, Co. Meath.	W.
1706.	**Muskins,**	Isaac, alderman, Kilkenny.	W.
1727.	**Myhill,**	Jane, widow, Dublin.	W.
1707.	**Naghten,**	Bartholomew, Loughboy, near Dublin.	W.
1813.	,,	Bernard, Drum, Co. Roscommon.	W.
1729.	**Nally,**	William, merchant, Dublin.	W.
1664.	**Nangle,**	Arthur, Kilbixy, Co. Westmeath.	W.
1741.	**Napper,**	William, Billsborough, Co. Meath.	G.

IRISH WILLS: COPIES AND ABSTRACTS.

Date of Probate.		REFERENCE
1813.	**Nash,** Arthur, Lame, Co. Mayo.	W.
1818.	,, Edward, Castlebar, Co. Mayo.	W.
1804.	**Nason,** Elizabeth, Youghal, Co. Cork.	G.
1736.	,, William, Rahenity, Co. Cork.	G.
1740.	,, William, merchant, Cork.	G.
1728.	**Naylor,** Jonathan, Rathmeen, Co. Wicklow.	W.
1818.	**Neale,** Abraham, Christianstown, Co. Kildare.	W.
1624.	,, Barbara, widow, Kinsale, Co. Cork.	G.
1683.	**Needham,** Symon, Ballycarroll, Queen's Co.	W.
1729.	,, Thomas, Crownehorne, Co. Wicklow.	W.
1728.	**Neigans,** Henry, sugar-baker, Belfast.	W.
1472.	**Neill,** William, Clondalkin, Co. Dublin.	T. & B., p.97.
1818.	,, William, Tralee, Co. Kerry.	W.
1818.	**Nettles,** Lieut. Henry, Clonmell.	W.
1728.	,, John, Foureen, Co. Waterford.	W.
1727.	,, Martha, widow.	W.
1727.	**Nevill,** Francis, Belturbet, Co. Cavan.	W.
1682.	,, Richard, Gt. Fornaghts, Co. Kildare.	W.
1728.	**Newburgh,** Henry, Raheck, Co. Cavan.	W
1706.	**Newenham,** John, Cork.	G.
1735.	,, John, clothier, Cork.	G.
1725.	,, Thomas, Cork.	G.
1766.	,, Thomas, Co. Cork.	G.
1759.	,, Richard, merchant, Cork.	G.
1731.	**Newman,** Charles, Kilshanig, Co. Cork	G,
1662.	,, Edward.	G.
1717.	,, Elizabeth, widow, Cork.	G.
1728.*	,, John, apothecary, Kinsale, Co. Cork.	G.
1755.	,, John, fisherman, Kinsale, Co. Cork.	G.
1787.	,, Philip, Kinsale, Co. Cork.	G.
1693.	,, Richard, Cork.	G.
1728.	,, Roger, farmer, Corballis, Co. Dublin.	W.
1726.	**Newstead,** Catherine, widow, Dublin.	W.
1727.	**Nicholson,** William, Archbishop of Cashel.	W.
1726.	**Nicolas,** Charles, Dublin.	W.

IRISH WILLS: COPIES AND ABSTRACTS.

Date of Probate.		REFERENCE.
1708.	**Nisbitt,** Andrew, Brenter, Co. Donegal.	W.
1670.	**Noell,** Sir Martin, Kt., Ballyhinch, Co. Kilkenny.	W.
1726.	**Norman,** Elizabeth, widow, Londonderry.	W.
1727.	**Norris,** William, Dublin.	W.
1726.	**North,** John, ribbon-maker, Earl-St., Dublin.	W.
1729.	,, Joseph, Newcastle, Co. Meath.	W.
1813.	**Nowlan,** William, tallow-chandler, Dublin.	W.
1793.	**Nugent,** Elinor, widow, Donore, Co. Westmeath.	N. v. 151, p.115.
1474.	,, Margaret, widow of Sir Thomas Newbery, Kt.	T. & B., p.80.
1813.	,, Oliver, Bobs Grove, Co. Cavan.	W.
1728.	,, Walter, Carpenterstown, Co. Westmeath.	W.
1727.	**Nuttal,** Charles, Boolybeg, Co. Kildare.	W.
1728.	**Oates,** Thomas, surgeon, Lisburn, Co. Antrim.	W.
1478.	**Obern,** Margaret.	T. & B., p.104.
1665.	**O'Brien,** Cuogher, Coylnocorry, Co. Cork.	W.
1742.*	,, Henry, Mallow, Co. Cork.	G.
1813.	,, Henry, Ballyglissan, Co. Cork.	W.
1813.	,, John, Foonagh, Co. Clare.	W.
1729.	,, Margaret, widow, Carrickfergus.	W.
1813.	,, Mary, widow, Dublin.	W
1707.	,, William, Kilmacahill, Co. Cork.	W. & G.
1859.*	,, William, Kanturk, Co. Cork.	C.
1769.	**O'Bryen,** Gertrude, widow, Cork.	G.
1640.	,, William, Coylnacurra, Co. Cork.	G.
1708.	,, William, clothier, Cork.	G
1730.	**O'Bryne,** William, Bealavaddy, Co. Cork.	G.
1680.	**O'Callaghane,** Cahir, Curra, Co. Cork.	G.
1727.	**O'Connell,** Maurice, Newtown.	W.
1783.	**O'Connor,** Hugh, merchant, Dublin.	N. v. 153, p.138.
1815.*	,, Hugh, Dublin and Bath.	N. v. 153, p.169.
1803.	,, Thomas, Woodquay, Co. Galway.	N. v. 153, p.138.
1814.	,, Valentine, merchant, Dublin.	N. v. 153, p.168.
1656.	**Odell,** Christopher, lieut.	G.
1761.	,, John, Bealdurogy, Co. Limerick.	G.
1790.	,, John, Ballinarugie, Co. Limerick	G.

IRISH WILLS: COPIES AND ABSTRACTS.

Date of Probate.		REFERENCE.
1701.*	**Odell,** Richard, College of Dublin.	G.
1801.	**Odlum,** William, Malahide, Co. Dublin.	G.
1813.	**O'Donnell,** Sir Neal, Newport Pratt, Co. Mayo.	W.
1813.	,, Simon, Deerpark, Co. Clare.	W.
1813.	**O'Donoghue,** Morgan, butter buyer, Cork.	W.
1729.	**Ogle,** Thomas, merchant, Dublin.	W.
1813.	**O'Grady,** Rev. Richard, Springfield, Co. Clare.	W.
1797.	**O'Harroran,** Thady, Ballycuneen, Co. Clare.	M. v. XII, 363.
1720.	**O'Hea,** James, Kilkeiran, Co. Cork.	G.
1813.	**O'Leary,** Catherine, spinster, Cork.	W.
1665.	**Olphert,** John, quartermaster to Major George Rawdon's troop.	W.
1670.	**O'Neill,** Bryan, Backistown, Co. Dublin.	G.
1804.*	,, Elizabeth, alias **Jones,** widow, Dublin.	G.
1738.	,, Henry, merchant, Dublin.	G.
1727.	,, James, Mullagh, Co. Cavan.	W.
1739.	,, John, Edenduff, Co. Antrim.	G.
1813.	,, Mary, Dublin.	W.
1813.	,, Myles, Arklow, Co. Wicklow.	W.
1728.	,, Neal, Tauriaghmore East, Co. Antrim.	W. & G.
1728.	,, Rose, widow, Dublin.	W.
1729.	,, Tully, Balbriggan, Co. Dublin.	W.
1813.	**O'Neille,** Cornelius, lime manufacturer, Youghal, Co. Cork.	W.
1729.	**Onge,** Abel, merchant, Dublin.	W.
1729.	**Ormsby,** Conway.	W.
1813.	,, John, Gortner Abbey, Co. Mayo.	W.
1727.	**Orpin,** Thomas, glazier, Carrickfergus.	W.
1851.	**Orr,** Mary, widow, Innishannon, Co. Cork.	G.
1842.	,, Sarah, widow, Sydney, N.S. Wales.	G.
1842.	,, William, M.D., Innishannon, Co. Cork.	G.
1696.	**Orrery,** Margaret, Dowager Countess of.	G.
1682.	,, Roger, Earl of.	W. & G.
1813.	**Osborne,** Edward.	W.
1708.	,, Henry, Dardistown, Co. Meath.	W.
1726.	,, John, Grangegorman-lane, Dublin.	W.
1683.	,, Robert, Londonderry.	W.

IRISH WILLS: COPIES AND ABSTRACTS.

Date of Probate.		REFERENCE.
1813.	**Osborne,** William, jeweller, Dublin.	W.
1813.	**O'Shee,** Mathew, Nicholstown, Co. Kilkenny.	W.
1727.	**Ossett,** George, brazier, Dublin.	W.
1813.	**Ossory,** John, Bishop of.	W.
1813.	**Ottiwell,** Henry, Dublin.	W.
1475.	**Outlawe,** Thomas, Ballymadun.	T. & B., p.30.
1813.	**Overend,** George, merchant, Dublin.	W.
1733.	**Owen,** Edward, Kilmore, Co. Monaghan.	G.
1739.	,, Henry, Ballindrumney, Co. Meath.	G.
1778.	,, Henry, Ballydrumney, Co. Meath.	G
1696.	,, John, Dublin.	G.
1765.	,, Mary, widow.	G.
1761.	,, Nicholas, Rathconnell, Co. Monaghan.	G.
1708.	**Packenham,** Anne, widow, Bracklin, Westmeath.	W.
1682.	**Page,** Edward, merchant, Dublin.	W.
1729.	**Pageitt,** William, Dublin.	W.
1683.	**Pakenham,** Philip, Dublin.	W.
1726.	**Palin,** John, farmer, Christchurch-yard, Dublin.	W.
1813.	**Palles,** Andrew, Dublin.	W.
1726.	**Palliser,** William, Archbishop of Cashel.	W.
1690.	**Palmer,** Cassandra, widow.	N. v. 148, p.363.
1813.	,, George, Dublin.	W.
1729.	,, Henry, Parsonstown, King's Co.	W.
1476.	,, John.	T. & B., p.35.
1667.	,, Stephen, vintner, Dublin.	W.
1729.	,, Thomas, Carrowmore, Co. Mayo.	W.
1727.	,, William, Dublin.	W. & G.
1765.	,, William, Dublin.	G.
1726.	**Parke,** Roger, Dunally, Co. Sligo.	W.
1727.	**Parker,** Elizabeth, Cork.	W.
1726.	,, Roger, Dublin.	W.
1706.	,, Vernon.	W.
1727.	**Parnell,** John, one of the Justices of the King's Bench.	W.
1738.	**Parr,** Edward, innholder, Cork.	G.
1744.*	,, Martha, Dingle, Co. Kerry.	G.

IRISH WILLS: COPIES AND ABSTRACTS.

Date of Probate.		REFERENCE
1771.*	**Parr,** Mary, widow, Dingle, Co. Kerry.	G.
1742.*	,, William, Dingle, Co. Kerry.	G.
1644.	**Parsons,** Lady Anne, late of Birr, King's Co.	W. & G.
1673.	,, Lowther, Birr, King's Co.	G.
1783.	,, Mary Ann, widow, Pembrokestown, Co. Cork.	G.
1651.	,, Sarah, Kinsale, Co. Cork.	G.
1705.	,, William, Tomduff, Co. Wexford.	G.
1737.	,, William, St. John's, Wexford.	G.
1708.	**Parvey,** Adam, Mountrath, Queen's Co.	W.
1813.	**Parvisol,** Elizabeth, alias **Orge,** widow, Dublin.	W.
1729.	**Passley,** James, joiner, Stradbally, Queen's Co.	W.
1778.	**Patrickson,** Ann, widow, Cork.	G.
1775.	,, Thomas, Grange, Co. Cork.	G.
1813.	**Patten,** Elenor, widow, Dublin.	W.
1707.	**Paul,** Mehetable, widow, Rathmore, Co. Carlow.	W
1726.	**Pavey,** John, Strahert, Co. Wexford.	W.
1665.	**Pawlett,** John, Dublin.	W.
1475.	**Payn,** Jacoba, alias **Kyng.**	T. & B., p.157.
1726.	**Payzant,** Lewis, Dublin.	W.
1721.	**Pearce,** John, Kilbree, Co. Cork.	G.
1677.	,, Nicholas, Ballyhaunder, Cork.	G.
1813.	**Peard,** Arabella, widow, Cork.	W.
1738.	**Pearde,** Henry, Coole, Co. Cork.	G.
1727.	**Pearse,** Daniel, alderman, Cork.	W.
1665.	,, James, Galway.	W.
1801.	**Peirce,** George, cordwainer, Blackpool, Co. Cork.	G.
1771.	,, Robert, merchant, Kinsale, Co. Cork.	G.
1772	,, Roger, pawnbroker, Cork.	G.
1667.	**Peisley,** Sir Francis, Kt., Roscrea, Co. Tipperary.	W.
1727.	**Pellesier,** Abel, Dublin.	W.
1711.	**Pembroke,** William, cardmaker, Cork.	G.
1727.	**Pennefather,** Anthony, Cappoquin, Co. Waterford.	W.
1667.	**Pennington,** John, malster, Dublin.	W.
1813.	**Peppard,** James, Gorey, Co. Wexford.	W.
1726.	**Peppard,** Robert, Kerdiffstown, Co. Kildare.	W.

IRISH WILLS: COPIES AND ABSTRACTS.

Date of Probate.			REFERENCE.
1713.	**Perceval,** Charles, Callon, Co. Kilkenny.		G.
1674.*	**Percevall** George, Dublin.		G.
1688.	,,	Hugh, Gortadrommough, Co. Clare.	G.
1693.	,,	John, tailor, Dublin.	G.
1745.	,,	Martha, widow.	G.
1653.	,,	Sir Philip, Kt.	G.
1710.*	**Percival,** Charles.		G.
1714.	,,	Edmond, Ballydinane, Co. Cork.	G.
1685.*	,,	Edward, pewterer, Dublin.	G.
1737.	,,	John, Wexford.	G.
1734.	,,	William, Dean of Emly.	G.
1813.	,,	William, Williamstown, Co. Wexford.	W.
1681.	**Percivall,** Dame Catherine widow.		W. & G.
1719.	,,	David, merchant, Dublin.	G.
1737.	,,	Edward, clerk, Clonkeen, Co. Louth.	G.
1656.	,,	Elizabeth, or **Persevall,** widow.	G.
1652.	,,	Hugh, merchant, Kinsale, Co. Cork.	G.
1688.	,,	Hugh Gortadrommough, Co. Clare.	W.
1718.	,,	John, Knightsbrook, Co. Meath.	G.
1703.	,,	Thomas, alderman, Drogheda.	G.
1747.	,,	Rev. William, Aghanlow, Co. Derry.	G.
1682.	**Percivell,** Mary, widow, Bandonbridge, Co. Cork.		G.
1682.	**Percy,** Joseph, glover, Dublin.		W.
1607.	**Percyvall,** Christopher, merchant, Dublin.		G.
1768.	**Perkins,** John, Dublin.		G.
1781.	,,	John Ballintraine, Co. Carlow.	G.
1794.	,,	Theophilus, Dublin.	G.
1801.	,,	William, carpenter, Grangebeg, Co. Kildare.	G.
1752.	**Perrie,** Ann, widow, Cork.		G.
1813.	**Perry,** Margaret, Clandy, Co. Tyrone.		W.
1619.	,,	Philip, Kilbrogan.	G.
1673.	**Persevall,** Mathias, Bandon, Co. Cork.		G.
1793.	**Peyton,** Isaac, silkweaver, Coombe, Dublin.		N. v. 151, p.115.
1741.	,,	John, Laughen, Co. Leitrim.	N. v. 148, p.129.
1796.	,,	Toby, Lagheen, Co. Leitrim.	N. v. 148, p.129.

Date of
Probate.

REFERENCE.

1786.	**Phair,** Edward, Waterford.	G.
1825.	,, Elizabeth, Millview, Co. Cork.	G.
1838.	,, William, Brook Lodge, Co. Cork.	G.
1762.	**Phaire,** Aldworth, St. John's, Co. Wexford.	G.
1752.	,, Alexander, St. John's, Co. Wexford.	G.
1761.	,, John, slater, Cork.	G.
1769.	,, Joseph.	G.
1768.	,, Mary, St. John's, Co. Wexford.	G.
1682.	,, Robert, Grange, Co. Cork.	W.
1749.	,, Thomas, Enniscorthy, Co. Wexford.	G.
1778.	,, Thomas, Enniscorthy, Co. Wexford.	G.
1728.	**Phillips,** Chichester, Dublin.	W.
1727.	,, Gertrude, spinster, Drogheda.	W.
1666.	,, William. Dublin.	W.
1669.	**Philpot,** Edward, Belturbet, Co. Cavan.	W.
1787.	**Philpott,** Usher, Cork.	G.
1726.	**Pickeaver,** Joseph, periwig-maker, Dublin.	W.
1742.*	**Pierce,** Edward, merchant, Cork.	G.
1748.	,, James, Dublin.	G.
1724.*	,, Joan, widow, Kinsale, Co. Cork.	G.
1750.	,, John, Whitestown, Co. Wexford.	G.
1732.	,, Richard, Ballinagaragh, Co. Kerry.	G.
1721.	,, Robert, Ballygromans, Co. Cork.	G.
1763.	**Pierse,** John, Dublin.	G.
1787.	,, or **Pierce,** Mary, widow, Cork.	G.
1761.	,, Richard, Foxhall, Co. Limerick.	G.
1772.	,, Richard, Tralee, Co. Kerry.	G.
1734.	,, Thomas, Ballinagaragh, Co. Kerry.	G.
1711.	**Piersy,** George, Shandon, Co. Cork.	G.
1685.	,, James, Shandon, Co. Cork.	G.
1764.	,, James, merchant, Cork.	G.
1626.	,, Richard, Shandon, Co. Cork.	G.
1681.	**Pigott,** Alexander, Innishannon, Co. Cork.	W. & G.
1726.	,, Benjamin, mariner.	W.
1763.	,, Emanuel, Cork	G.

IRISH WILLS: COPIES AND ABSTRACTS.

Date of Probate.		REFERENCE.
1773.	**Pigott,** George, Cork.	G.
1728.	,, John, Brockley, Co. Somerset.	W.
1729.	,, Thomas, Bannahery, Queen's Co.	W.
1729.	**Pimm,** Tobias, clothier, Edenderry, King's Co.	W.
1726.	**Pinkney,** Joseph, sawyer, Dublin.	W.
1662.	**Pitt,** Simon, alderman, Londonderry.	G.
1666.	,, or **Pitts,** Thomas, merchant, Stokestown.	G.
1706.	**Pitts,** Charles, Dublin.	W.
1704.*	,, Richard, alderman, Drogheda.	G.
1729.	**Pleasants,** Thomas, alderman, Dublin.	W.
1766.	**Plowman,** William, Grangebeg, Co. Kildare.	G.
1798.	,, William, Newtown, Co. Kildare.	G.
1728.	**Plummer,** Daniel, Castlequin, Co. Limerick.	W.
1463.*	**Plunket,** Sir Christopher, Kt.	J. v. VI, 357.
1681.	,, Ellinor, alias **Birmingham,** widow.	W.
1683.	,, Luke, Portmarnock, Co. Dublin.	W.
1682.	**Plunkett,** Francis, Mote, Co. Meath.	W.
1728.	,, Thomas, Portmarnock, Co. Dublin.	W.
1682.	**Poe,** William, Manor Poe, Co. Fermanagh.	W.
1726.	**Poirier,** or **Poiriez,** Lewis, merchant, Lisburn, Co. Antrim.	W.
1729.	**Pollard,** William, Royal Hospital, Dublin.	W.
1752.	**Pomeroy,** Thomas, Palace, Co. Cork.	G.
1667.	**Poore,** Nicholas, trumpeter to Earl Drogheda's Troop of Horse.	W.
1727.	**Porter,** Mary Anne, spinster, Dublin.	W.
1729.	,, Mary, widow, Dublin.	W.
1813.	,, Michael, Ballyhorsey, Co. Wicklow.	W.
1472.	,, Richard.	T. & B., p.44.
1706.	**Potter,** Allen, distiller, Dublin.	W.
1762.	,, Thomas, Fartha, Co. Cork.	G.
1666.	,, William, Dublin.	W.
1683.	**Powell,** Benjamin, merchant, Waterford.	W.
1813.	**Power,** Mary, widow, alias **Merry,** Waterford.	W.
1679.	,, Miles, Kilkenny.	G.
1813.	,, Nicholas, Waterford.	W.
1684.	,, Richard, Carrigline, Co. Cork.	G.

IRISH WILLS: COPIES AND ABSTRACTS.

Date of Probate.			REFERENCE.
1706.	**Power,** Richard, Ballindrummy, Co. Galway.		W.
1474.	,, William.		T. & B., p.94.
1707.	**Poyntz,** Lucas, Acton, Co. Armagh.		W.
1813.	**Pratt,** Jeremiah, port surveyor, Kinsale, Co. Cork.		W.
1706.	**Price,** Edward, Limerick.		W.
1706.	,, V. Rev. Henry, Dean of Cashel.		W.
1683.	,, James, Pilleth, Radnorshire.		W.
1688.	,, John, weaver, Bandon, Cork.		G.
1683.	,, Margaret, widow, Pilleth, Radnorshire.		W.
1712.	,, Richard, Ballyhooly, Co. Cork.		G.
1668.	,, Thomas, malster, Cork.		G.
1706.	,, Major Thomas, Dublin.		W.
1699.	,, William, Cork.		G.
1727.	**Prine,** Thomas, farmer, Portland, Co. Tipperary.		W.
1726.	**Prior,** Richard, Cambridge, Cambridgeshire.		W.
1726.	**Proby,** Rev. Charles, Damastown, Co. Dublin.		W. R. v. 28, pt. 1. E. p.101.
1726.	**Pugh,** Hugh, merchant, Dublin.		W.
1667.	**Pullein,** Samuel, Archbishop of Tuam.		W.
1727.	**Pullman,** Thomas, tallow chandler, Dublin.		W.
1744.*	**Purcell,** John, Gortinard, Co. Cork.		G.
1683.	,, Robert, Dublin.		W.
1758.	,, Thomas, Gortinard, Co. Cork.		G.
1728.	,, William, Kanturk, Co. Cork.		W.
1756.	,, William, Park, Co. Cork.		G.
1776.*	**Purdon,** Bartholomew.		G.
1745.*	,, Helena, widow.		G.
1741.	,, John, Dyshart, Co. Cork.		G.
1707.	**Purefoy,** Gamebel, Clanbullock, King's Co.		W.
1666.	**Purfield,** Christian, alias **Warren,** widow, Co. Dublin.		W.
1801.	,, Esther, widow, Dublin.		N. v. 151, p.115.
1775.	,, Thomas, baker, Dublin.		N. v. 154, p.168.
1682.	**Pyke,** John, senior, Woodenstown, Co. Tipperary.		W.
1796.	**Pyne,** Elizabeth, spinster, Dunmanway, Co. Cork.		G.
1674.	,, Henry, Ballyneglass, Co. Cork.		G.

IRISH WILLS: COPIES AND ABSTRACTS.

Date of Probate.		REFERENCE.
1713.	**Pyne,** Henry, Waterford, Co. Cork.	G.
1690.	,, John, Youghal, Co. Cork.	G.
1747.	,, Katherine, Dublin.	G.
1604.*	,, Nicholas.	G.
1711.	,, Sir Richard, Kt.	G.
1813.	**Queade,** Rev. Hayes, Kilgobbin, Co. Dublin.	W.
1728.	**Questerbrune,** Rev. John, Vicar of Burnchurch, Dioc. Ossory.	W.
1728.	**Quin,** Francis, bricklayer, Dublin.	W.
1726.	**Quooly,** Martin, merchant, Dublin.	W.
1729.	**Racine,** Anne, widow, Dublin.	W.
1726.	**Rafter,** Ignatius, Kilkenny, late of Dublin.	W.
1708.	**Rainsey,** or **Rayney,** Hugh, Maghrefelt, Co. Londonderry.	W.
1813.	**Rawlins,** Ann, widow, Dublin.	W.
1813.	,, Rev. William, Dublin.	W.
1729.	**Ray,** Mary, spinster, Dublin.	W.
1726.	**Raymond,** Rev. Anthony, Trim, Co. Meath .	W.
1764.	,, John, Mallow, Co. Cork.	G.
1727.	**Read,** James, Tolloghin, Co. Down.	W.
1682.	**Reade,** Alleyn, merchant tailor, London.	W.
1726.	**Reader,** William, apothecary, Dublin.	W.
1727.	**Reading,** Otway, Borrisoleigh, Co. Tipperary.	W.
1726.	**Reddrop,** Dorothy, widow, Dublin.	W.
1813.	**Redfoord,** Walter.	W.
1813.	**Redmond,** Elizabeth, widow, Dublin.	W.
1799.	**Reid,** Rev. James, Midleton, Co. Cork.	G.
1813.	,, James, distiller, Dundalk, Co. Louth.	W.
1629.	**Reignolds,** Henry, Dublin.	N. v. 149, p.364.
1729.	**Reilly,** Charles, alias **Cahire,** Aughuwee, Co. Cavan.	W.
1813.	,, Elizabeth, widow, Kilmore, Co. Cavan.	W.
1813.	,, Gerald, Ballinlagh.	W.
1775.	,, Mary, widow, Killbogan, Co. Kildare.	N. v. 151, p.115.
1708.	**Render,** William, Doudstown, Co. Louth.	W.
1707.	**Revett,** Thomas, alderman, Galway.	W.
1788.	**Reynolds,** Andrew, silk-manufacturer, Dublin.	N. v. 151, p.222. M. v. VI, 285.
1823.	,, Andrew, Drumrott, Co. Derry.	N. v. 147, p.354.

IRISH WILLS: COPIES AND ABSTRACTS.

Date of
Probate.

Date			Reference
1796.	**Reynolds,** Ann, spinster, Cornell's Court.		N. v. 154, p.170
1812.	,,	Bryan, Drumgowla, Co. Leitrim.	N. v. 149, p.296
1768.	,,	Catherine, Cloontumpher, Co. Leitrim.	N. v. 149, p.293
1636.*	,,	Charles, Seaghan, Co. Leitrim.	N. v. 146, p.245
1702.	,,	Charles, Seaghan, Co. Leitrim.	N. v. 151, p.4.
1706.	,,	Charles, Shick, Co. Leitrim.	N. v. 149, p.384
1751.	,,	Charles.	G.
1788.	,,	Charles.	N. v. 149, p.385
1800.	,,	Charles, Mohill, Co. Leitrim.	N. v. 149, p.295
1737.	,,	Christopher, baker, Dublin.	N. v. 151, p.131
1699.	,,	Daniel McTorlagh, Drumawnagh, Co. Leitrim.	N. v. 149, p.384
1775.	,,	Dorothy, alias **Ellis,** widow, Wardhouse.	N. v. 149, p.386
1788.	,,	Edmond, Derrylane, Co. Cavan.	N. v. 149, p.168
1770.*	,,	Edwyn Sandys, Durham, Co. Roscommon.	N. v. 148, p.365
1744.	,,	Francis, Curnafinowan, Co. Leitrim.	N. v. 149, p.293
1786.*	,,	Francis, farmer, Derrycree.	N. v. 149, p.168
1769.	,,	George, Grange, Co. Leitrim.	N. v. 149, p.385
1783.*	,,	George Nugent, Loughscur, Co. Leitrim.	N. v. 151, p.6.
1808.	,,	Henry, Trim, Co. Meath.	N. v. 149, p.169
1783.	,,	Hugh, farmer, Brianross, Co. Leitrim.	N. v. 149, p.294
1660.*	,,	Humphrey, Loughscur, Co. Leitrim.	N. v. 151, p.25
1769.	,,	James Dublin.	N. v. 151, p.132
1781.	,,	James, farmer, Co. Leitrim.	N. v. 149, p.294
1784.	,,	James, Cavan, Co. Leitrim.	N. v. 149, p.294
1796.*	,,	James, Annahavil, Co. Derry.	N. v. 147, p.354
1741.	,,	Jane, spinster, Dublin.	N. v. 151, p.131
1724.	,,	Jeffery.	N. v. 149, p.169
1759.	,,	Joan, widow, Dublin.	N. v. 150, p.403
1678.	,,	John, Rostrevor, Co. Down.	N. v. 149, p.365
1680.*	,,	John, Clogher, Co. Tyrone.	N. v. 149, p.365
1699.	,,	John, Loughscur, Co. Leitrim.	N. v. 151, p.25
1776.	,,	John, late of Dublin, now of Crumlin.	N. v. 148, p.364
1777.	,,	John, Drumcrommon, Co. Leitrim.	N. v. 151, p.6.
1782.	,,	John.	N. v. 149, p.169
1769.	,,	Laughlin, merchant, Creenagh, Co. Leitrim.	N. v. 149, p.293

IRISH WILLS: COPIES AND ABSTRACTS.

Date of Probate.			REFERENCE.
1761.	**Reynolds,** Letitia, widow, Magherychar, Co. Donegal.		N. v. 149, p.385.
1766.	,,	Margaret, widow, Dublin.	N. v. 151, p.132.
1769.	,,	Mary, alias **Waugh,** Drumlakill, Co. Leitrim.	N. v. 149, p.293.
1791.	,,	Mary, widow, Clonfad, Co. Roscommon.	N. v. 149, p.167.
1819.	,,	Mary.	N. v. 151, p.133.
1736.	,,	Michael, baker, Coomb, Dublin.	N. v. 151, p.131.
1772.	,,	Michael, Corregresse, Co. Leitrim.	N. v. 149, p.294.
1800.	,,	Rev. Michael, Killtaighter, Co. Leitrim	N. v. 149, p.295.
1771.	,,	Owen, Cavan, Co. Leitrim.	N. v. 149, p.293.
1789.	,,	Owen, Rinn, Co. Leitrim.	N. v. 149, p.294.
1767.*	,,	Patrick, baker, Dublin.	N. v. 149, p.169.
1767.	,,	Patrick, carpenter, Dublin.	N. v. 151, p.132.
1785.	,,	Patrick, ribbon weaver, Dublin.	N. v. 149, p.169.
1787.	,,	Patrick, Toorasugh, Co. Leitrim.	N. v. 149, p.294.
1788.	,,	Patrick, baker, Coombe, Dublin.	N. v. 151, p.132.
1796.	,,	Patrick, Farnaught, Co. Leitrim.	N. v. 149, p.295.
1796.	,,	Patrick, The Manse, Co. Kildare.	N. v. 154, p.169.
1798.	,,	Patrick, Dublin.	N. v. 151, p.132.
1813.	,,	Patrick, attorney, Belfast.	W.
1782.	,,	Robert, farmer, Lemgelton, Co. Cavan.	N. v. 149, p.168.
1700.	,,	Roger, Pallinolis, Co. Roscommon.	N. v. 149, p.167.
1791.	,,	Rose, widow, Dromlish, Co. Longford.	N. v. 149, p.295.
1797.	,,	Rose, widow, Dublin.	N. v. 151, p.223.
1783.	,,	Stephen, Anghamore, Co. Leitrim.	N. v. 154, p.169.
1761.	,,	Thady, dealer, Ballagh, Co. Longford.	N. v. 149, p.293.
1556.*	,,	Thomas, Dublin.	N. v. 150, p.294.
1632.	,,	Thomas, Clunties, Co. Leitrim.	N. v. 151, p.5.
1777.	,,	Thomas, Dengan, Co. Meath.	N. v. 149, p.168.
1782.	,,	Thomas, silk manufacturer, Dublin.	N. v. 151, p.278. M. v. VI, 285.
1793.	,,	Thomas, merchant, Dublin.	N .v. 151, p.132.
1797.	,,	Thomas, Mohill, Co. Leitrim.	N .v. 149, p.295.
1768.	,,	Timothy, Drumleehill, Co. Leitrim.	N. v. 154, p.169.
1664.	,,	William, Curloughan, Co. Kilkenny.	W.
1726.*	,,	William, victualler, Dublin.	N. v. 149, p.169.
1735.*	,,	William, clothier, Dublin.	N. v. 150, p.403.

IRISH WILLS: COPIES AND ABSTRACTS.

Date of Probate.		REFERENCE.
1786.	**Reynolds,** William, Athboy, Co. Meath.	N. v. 149, p.168.
1821.	,, William, farmer, Drumrott, Co. Derry.	N. v. 147, p.854.
1727.	**Reyson,** John, alderman, Dublin.	W.
1818.	**Ribert,** Jack Philip, cook, Shanbally, Co. Cork	W.
1758.	**Rice,** John, Dingle, Co. Kerry.	G.
1726.	,, Dame Mary, widow.	W.
1672.	**Rich,** Stephen, Wexford.	G
1818.	**Richard,** Mary, widow, Dublin.	W.
1729.	**Richards,** Elizabeth, widow, Dublin.	W.
1761.	,, John, farmer, Glascarig, Co. Wexford.	G.
1818.	,, Solomon, Solsborough, Co. Wexford.	W.
1728.	**Richardson,** Rev. James, Londonderry.	W.
1663.	**Richman,** Richard, cooper, New Ross.	G.
1648.*	**Richmond,** alias **Shipward,** Ballimodan, Co. Cork.	G.
1709.	,, Elizabeth, spinster, Cork.	G.
1611.	,, John, alias **Shipward,** Castle Mauhowne, Co. Cork.	G.
1687.*	,, Prudence, alias **Shipward,** widow, Ringrone, Co. Cork.	G.
1713.	**Rickotts,** John, blacksmith, Cork.	G.
1737.*	,, John, goldsmith, Cork.	G.
1760.	,, Jonas, mariner, Cork.	G.
1770.	,, Thomas, cordwainer, Cork.	G.
1745.	,, William, merchant, Cork.	G.
1707.	**Riddell,** John, merchant, Newry, Co. Down.	W.
1691.	**Ridgway,** Henry, yeoman, Ballycarroll, Queen's Co.	G.
1745.	,, Samuel, shagweaver, Dublin.	G.
1818.	**Riky,** John, Dublin.	W.
1818.	**Roberts,** Henry, ironmonger, Stradbally, Queen's Co.	W.
1727.	,, John, Dublin.	W.
1726.	,, Lewis, Dublin.	W.
1707.	,, Richard, Dublin.	W.
1727.	,, William, merchant, Dublin.	W.
1729.	**Robertson,** Moab, linen-draper, Dublin.	W.
1801.	**Roche,** Benjamin, Fonthill, Co. Carlow.	G.
1706.	,, George, alderman, Limerick.	G.
1474.	,, John, Dublin.	T. & B., p.90.

IRISH WILLS: COPIES AND ABSTRACTS.

Date of Probate.		REFERENCE.
1664.	**Roche,** Philip, Kinsale, Co. Cork.	W.
1726.	**Rochett,** Lewis, merchant, Lisburn, Co. Antrim.	W.
1733.	**Rochford,** David, merchant, Cork.	W.
1727.	**Rochfort,** Robert, Dublin.	W.
1721.	**Rogers,** George, Lota, Co. Cork.	G.
1728.	,, Hannah, widow, Cork.	W.
1726.	,, Henry, innkeeper, Kill, Co. Kildare.	W.
1813.	,, John, Grange, Co. Louth.	W.
1729.	,, Linegar, widow, Dublin.	W.
1726.	,, Richard, Balgeen, Co. Meath.	W.
1726.	**Ross,** James, mariner, master of "Speedwell."	W.
1813.	**Roughan,** Daniel, Ennis, Co. Clare.	W.
1813.	**Rourke,** John.	W.
1813.	,, William, shopkeeper, Clane, Co. Kildare.	W.
1729.	**Rous,** Joseph, merchant, Dublin.	W.
1728.	**Rowan,** Rev. John, Ballynagappog, Co. Down.	W.
1665.	**Rowe,** John, Castledilling, Co. Kildare.	W.
1708.	,, John, Rathmore, Co. Meath.	W.
1696.	,, Nicholas, Ballyharty, Co. Wexford.	G.
1760.	,, Nicholas, Sweetman's Well, Co. Wexford.	G.
1687.	,, Richard, Ballyharty, Co. Wexford.	G.
1683.	**Rowles,** William, Dunganstown, Co. Wexford.	W.
1683.	,, William, Mullingar, Co. Westmeath.	W.
1724.	**Roycraft,** James, Bandon, Co. Cork.	G.
1742.	,, William, merchant ,Bandon, Co. Cork.	G.
1795.	**Ruble,** Edward, Ballycannon, Co. Cork.	G.
1790.	,, Philip, farmer, Knocknacurra, Co. Cork.	G.
1666.	**Ruby,** Edward, yeoman, Carrigrohan, Co. Cork.	G.
1708.	**Ruerke,** Edmund, vintner, Dublin.	W.
1813.	**Russell,** Deborah, widow.	W.
1728.	,, James, Dublin.	W.
1729.	,, John, Ballydavid, Co. Tipperary.	W.
1729.	,, John, Rutland, Co. Carlow.	W.
1442.	,, Philip, Dublin.	A. 1898, p.122.
1729.	,, Richard, Currihills, Co. Kildare.	W.

IRISH WILLS: COPIES AND ABSTRACTS.

Date of Probate.		REFERENCE.
1813.	**Ruthen,** Capt. John Trotter, Bath.	W.
1683.	**Ruxton,** Henry, Bective, Co. Meath.	W.
1682.	**Ryan,** Darby, Castlemartyr, Co. Cork.	W.
1813.	,, Elizabeth, widow, Parsonstown, King's Co.	W.
1648.	**Ryves,** Sir William, Kt., Booterstown.	Z. 1888, p.139.
1476.	**Sale,** Walter.	T. & B., p.77.
1708.	**Salmon,** Thomas, Clonmel, Co. Tipperary.	W.
1668.	,, William, Co. Meath.	W.
1681.	**Samborne,** Thomas, Kinsale, Co. Cork.	W.
1706.	**Sanderson,** Alexander, Drumkeevill, Co. Cavan.	W.
1726.	,, Alexander, Castle Sanderson, Co. Cavan.	W.
1729.	**Sandes,** Lancelot, Kilkevan, Queen's Co.	W.
1728.	**Sandwith,** Jeremiah, farmer, Aughfad, Co. Wexford.	W.
1708.	**Sandys,** Edwin, engraver, Dublin.	W.
1755.	,, Patrick, Dublin.	G.
1707.	**Santley,** Gwen, alias **Jones,** Dublin.	W.
1716.	**Sargent,** Robert, Castlegrace, Co. Tipperary.	A. v. 1876-78, p.327.
1667.	**Sarjeant,** Thomas, Dublin.	W.
1683.	**Sarsfield,** William, Lucan.	W.
1653.	**Savadge,** Henry, Dublin.	G.
1755.	**Savage,** Catherine, Gorgerry, Co. Down.	G.
1780.	,, Elizabeth, widow, Saintfield, Co. Down.	G.
1804.	,, Henry, Prospect, Co. Down.	G.
1732.	,, Hugh, Downpatrick, Co. Down.	G.
1773.	,, John, Dunturk, Co. Down	G.
1755.	,, Lucas, Lissize, Co. Down.	G.
1751.	,, Lucy, widow, Dublin.	G.
1729.	,, Margaret, widow, Dublin.	G
1718.	,, Mary, Dublin.	G
1771.	,, Patrick, Dublin.	G.
1784.	,, Patrick, attorney, Dublin.	G.
1717.	,, Philip, Chancellor of Exchequer in Ireland.	G.
1744.*	,, Rowland, bricklayer, Dublin.	G
1672.	,, Thomas, Kilgarvan.	G.
1733.*	,, William, Kirkistown, Co. Down.	G.

IRISH WILLS: COPIES AND ABSTRACTS.

Date of Probate.		REFERENCE
1741.	**Savary,** John, the elder, East Greenwich, Kent.	G.
1704.	**Savery,** Daniel, merchant, Mallow, Co. Cork.	G.
1730.	**Sayers,** Rev. Edward, Doneraile, Co. Cork	G.
1749.*	**Scaife,** Thomas, Finglas, Co. Dublin.	U.
1813.	**Scott,** Ann, widow, Cork.	W.
1638.*	,, Sir Richard, Kt., Dublin.	Y. Bundle, July, 1641-2.
1717.	**Scull,** Josiah, Ballynacree, Co. Tipperary.	G.
1813.	**Seaver,** Mary, widow, Dublin.	W.
1683.	**Segar,** Rev. Richard, Rector of Clonenagh, Queen's Co.	W.
1707.	**Segrave,** Francis, Dublin.	W.
1728.	,, Mary, widow, Dublin.	W.
1469.	**Selyman,** James, Dublin.	T. & B., p.7.
1643.*	**Senlhorus,** John, Tankerkey, Co. Armagh.	Y. Bundle, Jan., 1643-4.
1599.	**Senleger,** Sir Warham, Kt.	G.
1728.	**Sequela,** Stephen, Kilkenny.	W.
1721.	**Servatt,** Stephen, Kinsale, Co. Cork.	G.
1708.	**Seward,** John, Kilkannoway, Co. Cork.	G.
1757.	,, Matthew, Mallow, Co. Cork.	G.
1680.	,, Richard, Clashnegannuffe, Co. Cork.	G.
1702.	,, Robert, Corbeah, Co. Cork.	G.
1643.	,, Simon, late of Co. Cork, and now of Bristol.	G.
1475.	**Sex,** Alice, alias **Bull.**	T. & B., p.116.
1813.	**Shadwell,** Bridget, spinster, Ballinasloe, Co. Galway.	W.
1729.	**Shallcrosse,** James, Co. Kerry.	W.
1727.	**Shapland,** Ellen, widow, Wexford.	W. & G.
1704.	,, John, Wexford.	G.
1746.	**Sharman,** John, Grange, Co. Antrim.	G.
1706.	**Sharpe,** Anthony, clothier, Dublin.	W.
1813.	**Sharply,** Mary, widow, Phibsborough, Co. Dublin.	W.
1728.	**Shaw,** John, Ballytweedy, Co. Antrim.	W.
1729.	,, Richard, Ballyderry, Co. Tipperary.	W.
1813.	**Shea,** Emilia, spinster, Dublin.	W.
1703.	**Sheares,** Humphrey, apothecary, Cork.	G.
1664.	**Shee,** Ellen, alias **Dobbyn,** widow, Freinstown, Co. Kilkenny.	W.

IRISH WILLS: COPIES AND ABSTRACTS.

Date of Probate.		Reference
1813.	**Shee,** John, Kilkenny.	W.
1728.	**Sheehy,** Catherine, widow, Dublin.	W.
1813.	**Sheils,** John, Dublin.	W.
1711.	**Sheldon,** Anne, widow, Dublin.	G.
1677.	**Shelton,** John, alderman, Dublin.	M. vol. XI, 515.
1813.	**Shepard,** or **Sheperd,** John, Lisburn, Co. Antrim.	W.
1664.	**Shepheard,** Mathew, Killerick, Co. Catherlagh.	W.
1813.	**Sheppard,** Sarah, widow, Cork.	W.
1683.	**Sheridan,** Anne, widow, Hill Hall.	W.
1707.	**Sherlock,** Eustace, Drumlargin.	W.
1807.	,, Mary, widow, Dublin.	N. v. 153, p.170.
1726.	,, Patrick, Dublin.	W.
1667.	**Sherlocke,** Richard, farmer, Donamore, Co. Meath.	W.
1744.	**Shewcraft,** Henry, cooper, Cork.	G.
1702.	,, John, yeoman, Ballynamona, Co. Cork.	G.
1762.	,, John, cooper, Cork.	G.
1813.	**Shewell,** Margaret, spinster, Dundalk.	W.
1729.	**Shiell,** Patrick, M.D., Brendrum, Co. Mayo.	G.
1637.	**Shipward,** John, alias **Richmond,** Carrilucas, Co. Cork.	G.
1729.	**Shollcross,** Thomas, Bishop's Court, Co. Kildare.	W.
1682.	**Short,** Peter, merchant tailor, London.	W.
1666.	**Shuel,** Edward, Ardfert, Co. Kerry.	W.
1667.	**Shurley,** Arthur, Isfield, Sussex.	W.
1726.	**Sibbald,** Comfort, widow, Mallymeaghan, Co. Westmeath.	W.
1813.	**Sillery,** Jane, widow, Drogheda.	W.
1813.	**Sillito,** Rev. Robert, Graig, Co. Kilkenny.	W.
1666.	**Simons,** Richard, mariner, Dublin.	W.
1727.	**Simpson,** George, merchant, Wicklow.	W
1728.	**Sinclair,** Anne, widow, Strabane, Co. Tyrone.	W.
1726.	**Singleton,** Samuel, M.D., Dublin.	W.
1813.	**Sinnott,** or **Synoth,** Catherine, widow, Kilbride, Co. Wexford.	W.
1708.	,, Ellen, widow, Waterford.	W.
1727.	,, Richard, late Dublin, and now of Drumcondra.	W.
1726.	,, Thomas, Dublin.	W.
1813.	**Skell,** James, Dolphin's Barn, Dublin.	W.

IRISH WILLS: COPIES AND ABSTRACTS.

Date of Probate.			REFERENCE.
1728.	**Skelton,** John, Loughill, Co. Kilkenny.		W.
1604.	,,	William, Robertstown, Co. Meath.	W.
1729.	**Skeolan,** or **Skollan,** Edmond, Limerick.		W.
1726.	**Skiddy,** Francis, Dublin.		W.
1734.	**Sleigh,** Francis.		G.
1729.	**Smalle,** Caleb, merchant, Dublin.		W.
1726.	**Smalley,** Benjamin, merchant, Dublin.		W.
1667.	**Smart,** James, merchant, Newtown.		W.
1683.	,,	William, Cork.	W.
1707.	**Smith,** Benjamin, merchant, Dunlavin, Co. Wicklow.		W.
1758.	,,	Rev. Benjamin, Shronehill, Co. Tipperary.	G.
1669.	,,	Deborah, spinster, Dublin.	G.
1717.	,,	Edward, Clonelough, Co. Monaghan.	G.
1813.	,,	Edward, Dublin.	W.
1731.	,,	Henry, merchant, Dublin.	G.
1699.	,,	James, merchant, Londonderry.	G.
1665.	,,	John, Mahoran, Co. Cork.	G.
1671.	,,	John, Clonemare, Cork.	G.
1703.	,,	John, alderman, Dublin.	G.
1715.	,,	John, chandler, Cork.	G.
1734.	,,	John, Dunmanway, Co. Cork.	G.
1813.	,,	Rev. John, Lismacray, Co. Tipperary.	W.
1707.	,,	Richard, Dublin.	W.
1708.	,,	Robert, Newland, Co. Dublin.	W.
1629.	,,	Thomas, clothier, Bandonbridge, Co. Cork.	G.
1641.*	,,	Thomas, Gillabby, Co. Cork.	G.
1663.	,,	Thomas, Ballymodan, Co. Cork.	G.
1727.	,,	Thomas, alderman, Waterford.	W.
1813.	,,	Thomas, merchant, Birr, King's Co.	W.
1598.	,,	Walter.	G.
1673.	,,	William, Archdeacon of Armagh.	G.
1716.	,,	Rev. William, Loughgilly, Co. Armagh.	G.
1727.	**Smyth,** Sir Percy, Kt. Ballinatray, Co. Waterford.		G.
1706.	,,	Rev. Robert, clerk, Ballyloughloe, Co. Westmeath.	W.
1813.	**Sneyd,** Rev. William, Fort Frederick, Co. Cavan.		W.

IRISH WILLS: COPIES AND ABSTRACTS.

Date of Probate.		REFERENCE.
1683.	**Sollom,** Mary, widow, Dublin.	W.
1683.	**Southalck,** George, watchmaker, Dublin.	W
1813.	**Spaight,** Samuel, Lodge, Co. Clare.	W.
1746.	**Span,** Benjamin, Castleforbes.	G.
1727.	,, Richard, Dublin.	W.
1813.	**Sparrow,** Richard, Oakland, Co. Tipperary.	W.
1686.	**Spencer,** Captain Henry, Fromrah (or Gromragh), Co. Antrim.	G.
1711.	,, Henry, lieutenant in Major-General Wade's Regiment.	G.
1675.*	,, John, Kilkenny.	G.
1654.	,, Lawrence, Bandonbridge, Co. Cork.	G.
1734.	,, Nathaniel, Rinny, Co. Cork.	G.
1668.*	,, Richard, hosier, Youghal, Co. Cork.	G.
1726.	,, Richard, sword cutler, Dublin.	W.
1669.	,, William, shoemaker, Dublin.	G.
1569.	**Spenser,** John, Dublin.	G.
1711.	**Spiller,** Fernando, Ross.	G.
1753.	,, Ferdinand.	G.
1700.	,, Henry, captain in Sir John Hammer's Regiment.	G.
1737.	,, Margaret, widow, Bandon, Co. Cork.	G.
1737.	,, Thomas, Cloghnakilty, Co. Cork.	G.
1760.	,, William, Rosscarbery, Co. Cork.	G.
1813.	**Sproule,** Solomon.	W.
1634.*	**Squler,** Lewis, Cork.	G.
1813.	**Squire,** John.	W.
1813.	**Stack,** Rev. John.	W.
1666.	**Stacke,** Edmond, Dublin.	W.
1813.	**Stacpoole,** George, Cragbrian, Co. Clare.	W.
1726.	**St. Agnan,** Alexander.	W.
1707.	**Stamer,** George, Carnelly, Co. Clare.	W.
1684.	**Stamers,** George, Balnadee, Co. Cork.	G.
1684.	**Stamers,** George, Balinadee, Co. Cork.	G.
1651.	,, John, Bandonbridge, Co. Cork.	G.
1719.*	,, John, Radrought, Ballinadee, Co. Cork.	G.
1756.	**Stammers,** John, merchant, Bandon, Co. Cork.	G.
1770.*	,, Sarah, widow, Bandon, Co. Cork.	G.

IRISH WILLS: COPIES AND ABSTRACTS.

Date of Probate.		REFERENCE.
1673.	**Stampe,** Timothy, Co. Wexford.	S.
1665.	**Stanley,** Alson, alias, **Malpas,** widow, Dublin.	W.
1813.	,, John, apothecary. Drogheda.	W.
1683.	,, Richard, Clonead, King's Co.	W.
1686.	**Stannard,** Robert, clerk, Chancellor of Ferns.	G.
1813.	**Stannus,** Thomas, Portarlington, Queen's Co	W.
1665.	**Staples,** George, Dublin.	W.
1683.	**Staughton,** Richard, Dublin.	W.
1813.	**Staunton,** Patrick, Coolmane Lodge, Galway.	W.
1685.	**Stawell,** Anthony, Kinsale, Co. Cork.	Q., p.359.
1839.	,, Catherine, Kilbrack.	Q., p.362.
1825.	,, George, Summerhill, Co. Cork.	Q., p.366.
1691.	,, Jane, Kinsale, Co. Cork.	Q., p.360.
1716.	,, Jonas, Madam, Co. Cork.	Q., p.361.
1758.	,, Jonas, Mallow, Co. Cork.	Q., p.366.
1768.	,, Jonas, Kilbrittain, Co. Cork.	Q., p.361.
1821.	,, Sampson, Kilbrittain, Co. Cork.	Q., p.362.
1830.	,, William, Kilbrack.	Q., p.361.
1682.	**Steevens,** John, clerk, Athlone.	W.
1769.	**Stephens,** Edward, farmer, Paulville, Co. Carlow.	G.
1805.	,, Edward, Kilmuckaridge, Co. Wexford.	G.
1813.	**Sterling,** Mathew, Mount Browne, Co. Mayo.	W.
1727.	**Sternhert,** Thomas, victualler, Dublin.	W.
1665.	**Steuart,** Sir Robert, Kt., Kilmore, Co. Donegal.	W.
1481.	**Steven,** Joan, alias **Mastoke,** widow, Crumlin.	W.
1666.	**Stevenson,** William, saddler, Dublin.	T. & B., p.160.
1726.	**Stewart,** Andrew, quarter-master, Thurles, Co. Tipperary.	W.
1729.	,, George, Omagh, Co. Tyrone.	W.
1813.	,, George, Surgeon-General of Army in Ireland.	W.
1707.	,, James, Forth Cunningham, Co. Donegal.	W.
1726.	,, James, Killymoon, Co. Tyrone.	W.
1727.	,, Margaret, widow, Killymoon, Co. Tyrone.	W.
1729.	,, Hon. Richard, Dublin.	W.
1727.	,, Thomas, Dublin.	W.
1706.	,, William, Killymoon, Co. Tyrone.	W.

Date of
Probate.

1727. **Stewart,** William, Hanover-Square, London.	W.
1813. ,, William.	W.
1726. **St. George,** Henry, Athlone, Co. Roscommon.	W.
1726. ,, Richard, Drunmore, Co. Galway.	W.
1714. **Stiffe,** Samuel, mariner, Moyallow, Co. Cork.	G.
1457. **Stiward,** Ellen.	T. & B., p.2.
1729.* **St. Leger,** Andrew, Ballyvoholane, Co. Cork.	G.
1781. ,, Chichester, Doneraile, Co. Cork.	G.
1688. ,, Hayward, Cork.	G.
1790.* ,, Hayward, Cork.	G.
1788.* ,, Jane, spinster, Danesport, Cork.	G.
1696. ,, John, Doneraile, Co. Cork.	G.
1727.* ,, John, Cork.	G.
1738. ,, John, Kilkenny.	G.
1741.* ,, Sir John, Kt.	G.
1793. ,, Mary, alias **Butler,** widow.	G.
1738. ,, Robert, Newtown, Co. Kilkenny.	G.
1736. ,, Thomas, grocer, Dublin.	G.
1758. ,, Thomas, Dublin.	G.
1766. ,, Warham, Doneraile, Co. Cork.	G.
1784. ,, Warham, Cork.	G.
1729. **Stone,** George, merchant, Armagh.	W.
1624. **Stonehouse,** Alleson, Bellehinche, Co. Armagh.	Y. Reg. Test., 88, 116.
1707. **Stopford,** Joseph, lieutenant, Colonel Gorge's Regiment of Foot.	W.
1683. **Storer,** Anthony, draper, London.	W.
1707. **Stothard,** Thomas, pewterer, Cork.	W.
1707. **Stoyte,** Sir Francis, Kt., Dublin.	W.
1840. **Strangman,** Joseph, Waterford.	G.
1813. **Stratford,** Jane, widow, Dublin.	W.
1761. **Stuart,** Jane, widow, Dublin.	G.
1728. **Stubbs,** Martin, gardener, Co. Dublin.	W.
1729. **Styles,** William, merchant, Dublin.	W.
1813. **Swayne,** Benjamin, Cork.	W.
1724. **Sweeny,** Elizabeth, widow, Dublin.	G.
1806. ,, Roger, Dublin.	G.

IRISH WILLS: COPIES AND ABSTRACTS.

Date of Probate.			REFERENCE.
1728.	**Sweet,** Stephen, Kilkenny.		W.
1726.	**Sweetman,** John, Killadowan, Co. Kildare.		W.
1789.	**Sweny,** Michael, Woodbrookin, Co. Dublin.		G.
1741.	,,	Owen, Newmarket, Co. Dublin.	G.
1813.	,,	Thomas, Dublin.	W.
1707.	**Swinerton,** Richard, Lisburn, Co. Antrim.		W.
1797.	**Swiny,** Christina, Enniscorthy, Co. Wexford.		G.
1745.	,,	Daniel, Wexford.	G.
1760.	,,	Christine, widow, Dublin.	G.
1758.	,,	Mary, spinster, Dublin.	G.
1690.	,,	Rev. Miles, Wexford.	G.
1797.	,,	Rev. Shapland, Templeshannon, Co. Wexford	G.
1729.	,,	William, Ballyteige, Co. Wexford	G.
1781.	**Swyny,** Dermod, Currybehagh, Co. Cork		G.
1780.	,,	Francis, Two Pot House, Co. Cork.	G.
1702.*	,,	John, Killmurry, Co. Cork.	G.
1650.	**Swynye,** Terlogh, or Terence, Cork.		G.
1718.	**Symes,** Andrew, Ballymoney, Co. Cork.		G.
1698.	,,	George, Ballymodan, Co. Cork.	G
1731.	,,	Isabella, spinster, Cork.	G.
1667.	,,	Thomas, Dublin.	W.
1680.	**Symons,** William, tanner, Cork.		G.
1741.	**Synge,** Edward, Archbishop of Tuam.		G.
1710.	,,	Margaret, widow of Dean of Kildare	G.
1727.	**Synnot,** Jane, widow, Dublin.		W.
1707.	**Taaffe,** Edward, Dublin.		W.
1813.	,,	Julia, widow, Dublin.	W.
1707.	**Tabb,** Nicholas, currier, Limerick.		W.
1475.	**Tailor,** Philip.		T. & B., p.148.
1666.	**Talbot,** John, Drogheda.		W.
1667.	,,	Robert, M.D., Dublin.	W.
1688.	,,	William, Bodder, Co. Meath.	W.
1814.	**Tandy,** Burton, Drogheda.		G.
1793.	,,	Charles, Portobello, Co Dublin	G.
1812.	,,	Edward, Dublin.	G.

IRISH WILLS: COPIES AND ABSTRACTS.

1746.	**Tandy,** George, Drindally, Co. Meath.	G.
1798.	,, George, Lisburn, Co. Antrim.	G.
1805.	,, George, Dublin.	G.
1813.	,, George Edward, late of Dublin, now of Dawlish, Devon.	W. & G.
1784.	,, Henry, merchant, Waterford.	G.
1790.	,, James, merchant, Dublin.	G.
1741.	,, John, Drewstown, Co. Meath.	G.
1785.	,, John, Dublin.	G.
1775.	,, Joseph, Grange-o' Nelland, Co. Armagh.	G.
1800.	,, Marian.	G.
1684.	,, Thomas, Drewstown, Co. Meath.	G.
1739.	**Tanner,** Charles, chandler, Cork.	G.
1626.	,, James, Donguihie, Co. Limerick.	G.
1740.	,, Jonathan, senr., merchant, Bandon, Co. Cork.	G.
1776.	,, Jonathan, Bandon, Co. Cork.	G.
1711.	,, Katharine, widow, Ballynamuck, Co. Cork.	G.
1785.	,, Mary, widow, Annesville, Co. Cork.	G.
1727.	**Tate,** Samuel, Dunlady, Co. Down.	W.
1742.	**Tavener,** William, Cork.	G.
1715.	**Taverner,** Jacob, Limerick.	G.
1744.*	,, Samuel, Lissanode, Co. Westmeath.	G.
1707.	**Taylor,** Alice, alias **Partington,** widow, Dublin.	W.
1732.*	,, Berkeley, Ballynort, Co. Limerick.	G.
1665.	,, Edward, Tipperstown, Co. Kildare.	W.
1761.	,, Edward, Ballynort, Co. Limerick.	G.
1813.	,, Edward, Dublin.	W.
1784.	,, Elizabeth, widow, Dublin.	G.
1667.	,, Jeremy, Bishop of Down.	W.
1690.*	,, John, Bandonbridge, Co. Cork.	G.
1691.	,, John, Bandonbridge, Co. Cork.	G.
1714.	,, John, innkeeper, Cork.	G.
1728.	,, John, merchant, Belfast.	W.
1734.	,, John, Cork.	G.
1794.	,, John, farmer, Monycross, Co. Wexford.	G.
1884.	,, John.	G.

IRISH WILLS: COPIES AND ABSTRACTS.

Date of Probate.			REFERENCE.
1781.	**Taylor,** Joshua, cooper, Cork.		G.
1725.	,,	Judith, Ballynort, Co .Limerick.	G.
1726.	,,	Richard, Co. Down.	W.
1728.	,,	Samuel, Dublin.	W.
1728.	,,	Sarah, widow, Dublin.	W.
1682.	,,	Thomas, Dublin.	W.
1650.*	,,	William, innholder, London.	G.
1667.	,,	William, brewer, Dublin.	W.
1741.	,,	William, Boyerstown, Co. Meath.	G.
1846.	,,	William, Wexford.	G.
1727.	**Teague,** John, Dublin.		W.
1663.	**Tent,** Lieut. John, Cork.		W.
1746.	**Terry,** Sarah, spinster, Dublin.		G.
1767.	,,	Sarah, Cork.	G.
1692.	**Terrye,** Richard, maltster, Cork.		G.
1661.	**Thimelbee,** George, merchant, London.		W.
1680.	**Thomas,** Amy, widow, Ringrone, Co. Cork.		G.
1813.	,,	Francis, Hacketstown, Co. Carlow.	W.
1813.	**Thompson,** George, Dublin.		W.
1666.	,,	John, victualler, Christchurch-yard, Dublin.	W.
1664.	,,	or **Tomsone,** William, The Cavane, Donachmore.	W.
1681.	,,	or **Thomson,** William, merchant, Dublin.	W.
1813.	**Thornhill,** James Badham, Thornhill Lawn, Co. Limerick.		W.
1707.	**Thornton,** Isaac, Aughevenagh, Co. Cavan.		W.
1727.	**Throckmorton,** Theobald, Cullyhanna, Co. Armagh.		W.
1726.	**Thwaites,** Ephraim, maltster, Dublin.		W.
1729.	,,	Mary, widow, Dublin.	W.
1729.	,,	William, Dublin.	W.
1668.	**Tichborne,** Henry, ensign, Dublin.		W.
1667.	**Tichburne,** Sir Henry, Kt., Dublin.		W.
1813.	**Tighe,** Richard Grange, Gorman Lane, Dublin.		W.
1667.	**Tirconnell,** Oliver, Earl of.		W.
1732.	**Tirry,** William, Macrompe, Co. Cork.		G
1727.	**Tisdall,** Michael, Mount Tisdall, Co. Meath.		W.
1813.	**Todd,** Alexander, Dublin.		W.

IRISH WILLS: COPIES AND ABSTRACTS.

Date of Probate.		REFERENCE.
1727.	**Todd,** John, Ringclare, Co. Down.	W.
1706.	**Tomlinson,** Rev. Daniel, Philipstown, King's Co.	W.
1708.	,, Joan, widow, Dublin.	W.
1683.	**Tonge,** Rev. Thomas, D.D., New Ross.	W.
1702.	**Tooker,** William, Lisnagree, Co. Cork.	G.
1818.	**Toole,** Ann, alias **Reilly,** alias **Keating,** Dublin.	W.
1727.	**Towers,** Robert, brazier, Dublin.	W.
1707.	**Towills,** Bernard, clothier, Dublin.	W.
1762.	**Townsend,** Rev. Francis, Drishane, Co. Cork.	G.
1727.	**Tracey,** George, Tullamore, King's Co.	W.
1769.	**Traffe,** John, Stephenstown, Co. Louth.	G.
1754.	**Travers,** Boyle, Bandon, Co. Cork.	G.
1759.	,, Rev. Boyle, Dublin.	G.
1745.	,, Cassandra, widow, Dublin.	G.
1726.	,, Daniel, merchant, Dublin.	W. & G.
1712.	,, John, Cork.	G.
1727.	,, John, Bandon, Co. Cork.	W. & G.
1727.	,, Rev. John, Dublin.	W. & G.
1664.	,, Joseph, Archdeacon of Kildare.	W.
1728.	,, Robert, Coolconorthy, Co. Cork	G.
1758.	,, Robert, Mossgrove, Co. Cork.	G.
1726.	**Trench,** V. Rev. John, Dean of Raphoe.	W.
1475.	**Trevers,** Michael, Courtlough, Co. Dublin.	T. & B., p.117.
1726.	**Trevor,** Edward, Brynkinall, Denbighshire.	W.
1666.	**Trewsdall,** Francis, Dublin.	W.
1726.	**Trimble,** Michael, merchant, Dublin.	W.
1818.	**Trimlestown,** Nicholas, Lord Baron.	W.
1818.	**Troy,** Patrick, publican, Kilcoole, Co. Wicklow.	W.
1707.	**Truel,** John, carpenter of the "Royal Oak" man-of-war.	W.
1754.	**Tuam,** Jonah, Archbishop of.	G.
1638.*	**Tucker,** Andrew.	G.
1695.	,, Edward, merchant, Cork.	G.
1642.	,, John, Cork.	G.
1666.	**Tuite,** James, Dublin.	W.
1728.	,, Sir Joseph, Bart., Sonna, Co. Westmeath.	W.

IRISH WILLS: COPIES AND ABSTRACTS.

Date of Probate.		REFERENCE.
1726.	**Tumin,** John, surgeon, Westpanstown, Co. Dublin.	W.
1726.	**Turgge,** William, Archdeacon of Limerick.	W.
1633.	**Turner,** Edward, merchant, Balligobane, Co. Cork.	G.
1648.	,, Henry, burgess, Bandonbridge, Co. Cork.	G.
1653.	,, Major Henry, Bandonbridge, Co. Cork.	G.
1707.	,, Henry, Dublin.	W.
1728.	,, John, goldbeater, Dublin.	W.
1785.	,, John, Cork.	G.
1643.	,, Mary, widow, Cork.	G.
1679.	,, Sarah, Youghal, Co. Cork.	G.
1715.	,, William, miller, Limerick.	G.
1741.	,, William, burgess, Limerick.	G.
1813.	**Turnly,** Catherine, widow, Belfast.	W.
1666.	**Turnor,** Samuel.	W.
1728.	**Tyler,** Thomas, innholder, Dublin.	W.
1663.	**Tyllyer,** Henry, Island of Antigue.	W.
1692.	**Tynte,** Henry, Ballycrenan, Co. Cork.	M. V. XI, 511.
1746.*	**Tyrry,** Dominick, Macroom, Co. Cork.	G.
1669.	,, George Fitzwilliam, Cork.	G
1678.	,, Patrick, Ballynacrussy, Co. Cork.	G.
1578.	**Unake,** James, burgess, Youghal, Co. Cork	G.
1682.	**Uniacke,** James, Dublin.	W.
1733.	,, James, Mount Uniacke, Co. Cork.	G.
1730.	,, John, Curreheen, Co. Cork.	G.
1691.	,, Mary, widow, Dublin.	G.
1734.	,, Mary, spinster, Youghal, Co. Cork.	G.
1727.	,, Norman Curreheen, Co. Cork.	W. & G.
1777.	,, Norman, Castletown, Co. Cork.	G.
1761.*	,, Richard, late of Mount Uniacke, now of Youghal, Co. Cork.	G.
1734.	,, Thomas, Youghal, Co. Cork.	G.
1706.	**Upton,** Arthur, Castle Upton, Co. Antrim.	W.
1667.	**Urian,** Edward, King's Co.	W.
1476.	**Usberne,** Joan, Lusk.	T. & B., p.126.
1745.	**Uvedale,** Lieutenant Edmond.	G.
1728.	**Van Cruyskerchen,** Henry, merchant, Limerick.	W.

IRISH WILLS: COPIES AND ABSTRACTS.

Date of Probate.		REFERENCE.
1727.	**Vandeleur,** Rev. John, Kilrush, Co. Clare	W.
1665.	**Vanhoegaerden,** Abraham, merchant, Limerick.	W.
1728.	**Varangle,** John, Dublin.	W.
1683.	**Vaughan,** John, merchant, Youghal, Co. Cork.	W.
1727.	,, John, Dublin.	W.
1683.	**Verner,** Henry, Gilgavenagh, Co. Antrim.	W.
1682.	**Vesey,** Theodorus, clerk, Kinsale, Co. Cork.	W.
1813.	**Vicars,** Martha, Dublin.	W.
1707.	,, Richard, Garron M'Conly, Queen's Co.	W.
1729.	**Vigors,** Martha, widow, Dublin.	W.
1666.	**Vincent,** Thomas, Irishtown, Co. Dublin.	W.
1707.	**Vivers,** John, whitesmith, Dublin.	W.
1709.	**Vowell,** Rev. Christopher, Garrynegranogue, Co. Cork.	G.
1724.	,, Christopher, Ballyoran, Co. Cork.	G.
1735.	,, John, Springfort, Co. Cork.	G.
1681.	,, Richard, Castlelyons, Co. Cork.	G.
1813.	**Waddell,** Isabella, Springfield, Co. Down.	W.
1813.	,, Margaret, Springfield, Co. Down.	W.
1813.	,, Mary, spinster, Newforge, Co. Down	W.
1813.	**Waddle,** Elizabeth Ann, Curley, Co. Down	W.
1813.	,, Robert, Islanderry, Co. Down.	W.
1813.	**Wainwright,** William, Malton, Co. Wicklow	W.
1715.	**Wakeham,** John, Aghada, Co. Cork.	G.
1710.	,, Richard, Ballylegan, Co. Cork.	G.
1718.	,, William, Little Island, Co. Cork.	G.
1665.	**Wale,** Thomas, Dublin.	W.
1706.	**Walker,** George, Dublin.	W.
1683.	,, Jóhn, Dublin.	W.
1726.	,, John, Dundalk, Co. Louth.	W.
1685.	,, Thomas, Glassdargan, Co. Cork.	G.
1813.	,, Thomas, Richhill, Co. Armagh.	W.
1728.	**Wall,** Francis, merchant, Dublin.	W.
1813.	**Wallace,** Alexander, Newry, Co. Down.	W.
1780.	,, Hugh, Saintfield, Co. Down.	G.
1666.	,, John, merchant, Copper Alley, Dublin.	W.

IRISH WILLS: COPIES AND ABSTRACTS.

Date of Probate.		REFERENCE.
1791.	**Wallace,** Margaret, alias **Henderson,** alias **Savage,** widow.	G.
1813.	,, Richard, Coppenrush.	W.
1813.	,, William, merchant, Limerick.	W.
1813.	**Waller,** Lieut. Edward.	W.
1728.	**Walsh,** Charles, Derrilahan, Co. Tipperary.	W.
1813.	,, James, Dublin.	W.
1813.	,, James, breeches-maker, Dublin.	W.
1813.	,, Joseph, merchant, Waterford.	W.
1813.	,, Lucy, widow, Dublin.	W.
1664.	,, Martin, linen-draper, Dublin.	W.
1707.	,, Martin, maltster, Waterford.	W.
1708.	,, Mary, alias **Rourke,** widow, Dublin.	W.
1769.	,, Nicholas, linen-draper, Dublin.	N. v. 154, p.170.
1772.	,, Nicholas, corn-merchant, Dublin.	N. v. 151, p.206.
1813.*	,, Patrick, planter, Tartado of St. José, Sumidero.	C.
1474.	,, Robert.	T. & B., p.67.
1729.	**Warburton,** Mary, widow, Dublin.	W.
1813.	**Ward,** Hon. Edward, Castleward.	W.
1664.	,, Captain Henry.	W.
1708.	,, Mary, widow, Dublin.	W.
1681.	,, Michael, Bishop of Derry.	W.
1666.	,, Robert, Derryluskane, Co. Tipperary.	W.
1667.	**Warden,** William, Burchchurch, Co. Kilkenny.	W.
1666.	**Ware,** Sir James, Kt., Dublin.	W.
1665.	**Waring,** Thomas, Belfast.	W.
1707.	**Warneford,** Robert, Mountmellick, Queen's Co.	W.
1678.	**Warner,** Elizabeth, widow, Bandonbridge, Co. Cork.	G.
1682.	,, Henry, Lieut.-Col. to Maj.-Gen. Crawford.	W.
1813.	,, Henry, surgeon, Rathkeale.	W.
1748.	,, Mary, widow, Cork.	G.
1661.	,, Randall.	G.
1725.	,, Randall, Lissecrimeen, Co. Cork.	G.
1698.*	,, William, Ballymodan, Co. Cork.	G.
1726.	**Warren,** Catherine, alias **Aylmer,** widow.	W.
1679.	,, Henry, Dublin.	W.

IRISH WILLS: COPIES AND ABSTRACTS.

Date of Probate.		REFERENCE.
1707.	**Warren**, John, haberdasher, Dublin.	W.
1729.	,, John, merchant, Dubiln.	W.
1726.	,, Maurice, Dublin.	W.
1728.	,, Sarah, Corbalis, Co. Meath.	W.
1681.	**Warter**, Gamaliel, Bilboe, Co. Limerick.	W.
1818.	**Waterford**, Joseph Stock, Bishop of.	W
1666.	**Waterhouse**, Anne, widow, Dublin.	W.
1664.	,, Thomas, alderman, Dublin.	W.
1715.	**Watkins**, Abraham, Cork.	G.
1642.	,, Edward, Ballymodan, Co. Cork.	G.
1659.*	,, John, Kilbolane, Co. Cork.	G.
1687.	,, John, Bandonbridge, Co. Cork.	G.
1700.	,, John, Ballymee, Co. Cork.	G.
1699.	,, Margaret, Bandonbridge, Co. Cork.	G.
1729.	,, Mary, widow, Cork.	G.
1728.	**Watson**, Hannah, widow, Killister, Co. Dublin.	W.
1728.	,, Lancelot, merchant, Newry, Co. Down.	W.
1813.	,, Richard.	W.
1728.	,, William, farmer, Ballynamallagh, Co. Kildare.	W.
1688.	**Way**, John, Cork.	G.
1741.	**Wayes**, Peter, carpenter, Cork.	G.
1706.	**Webb**, Edward, linen-draper, Dublin.	W.
1707.	,, John, victualler, Dublin.	W.
1695.	**Webber**, Edward, alderman, Cork.	G.
1730.	,, Edward, Cork.	G.
1780.	,, Elizabeth, spinster, Cork.	G.
1784.	,, Ferdinando, organ-builder, Dublin	G.
1674.*	,, George, merchant, Cork.	G.
1682.	,, George, Skinner, Clonmel.	G.
1772.	,, George, Cork.	G.
1675.	,, Martha, widow, Cork.	G.
1666.	,, Michael, mariner, Cork.	G.
1669.	,, Michael, Cork.	G.
1749.	,, Michael, Cork.	G.
1786.*	,, Rev. Samuel, Baldoyle, Co. Dublin.	G.

IRISH WILLS: COPIES AND ABSTRACTS.

Date of Probate.		REFERENCE.
1785.	**Webber,** Susanna, widow, Cork.	G.
1678.	**Weekes,** John, Dublin.	G.
1802.	,, John, Attorney-at-Law, Dublin.	G.
1681.	,, Mark.	G.
1772.	,, Mary, widow, Cork.	G.
1788.	,, Mary Ann, widow, Cork.	G.
1789.	,, Nicholas, Ballynanty, Co. Limerick.	G.
1728.	,, Sarah, widow, Waterford.	W.
1777.	,, Thomas, Ashgrove, Co. Cork.	G.
1667.	,, William, Loughgur.	G.
1670.	,, William, Glonegar, Co. Limerick.	G.
1762.	**Weeks,** Nicholas, Councillor-at-Law, Cork.	G.
1729.	**Weld,** Thomas, merchant, Dublin.	W.
1729.	**Welsh,** or **Walsh,** Ally, widow, Ballymore, Co. Westmeath.	W.
1729.	,, Anthony, Lisburn, Co. Antrim.	W.
1667.	,, Thomas, Pilltown, Co. Waterford.	W.
1727.	,, Thomas, Q.M. in Col. Bowles' Regt. of Horse.	W.
1727.	,, William, farmer, Balraheen, Co. Kildare.	W.
1771.	**Welstead,** Christian, widow, Cork.	G.
1708.	,, John, Kilburne, Co. Cork.	G.
1666.	**Wentworth,** Sir George, Kt., Wentworth, Woodhouse, Yorks.	W.
1682.	**Wesley,** Garrett, Dangan, Co. Meath.	W.
1728.	,, Garrett, Dangan, Co. Meath.	W.
1813.	**West,** David, captain.	W.
1726.	,, James, Cranlamore, Co. Longford.	W.
1813.	,, Mary, spinster, Dublin.	W.
1729.	**Westby,** Nicholas.	W.
1474.	**Weston,** Reginald.	T. & B., p.90.
1726.	**Westropp,** Mountifort, Attyflin, Co. Limerick.	W.
1683.	**Wheaton,** William, St. Stephen's Green, Dublin.	W.
1710.	**Wheddon,** Thomas.	G.
1813.	**Wheleham,** Thomas, farmer, Castlejordan, Co. Meath.	W.
1476.	**Whitakyr,** Richard, Bremore, Co. Dublin.	T. & B., p.119.
1761.*	**Whitby,** Catherine, widow, Kilcregan, Co. Kilkenny.	G.
1751.	,, Edward, Kilcregan, Co. Kilkenny.	G.

IRISH WILLS: COPIES AND ABSTRACTS.

Date of Probate.			REFERENCE
1782.*	**Whitby,**	Elizabeth, Cloneyanch, King's Co.	G.
1694.*	,,	Helen, widow, Kilterman, Co. Tyrone.	G.
1776.	,,	Jonathan, Waterford.	G
1799.	,,	Jonathan, merchant, Castleblaney, Co. Monaghan.	G.
1658.	,,	Captain Marcus, Fermoy, Co. Cork.	G.
1684.	,,	Robert, Whitfield Town.	G.
1745.	,,	Robert, Kilcregan, Co. Kilkenny.	G.
1728.	**White,**	Alexander, Deigan, Co. Cavan.	W.
1813.	,,	Ann, Wicklow.	W.
1845.*	,,	Benjamin Newport, Cashel.	U.
1825.*	,,	Catherine, widow, Lisowen, Co. Limerick.	U.
1857.*	,,	Catherine Elizabeth, widow, Cashel.	U.
1755.*	,,	Frances, spinster, Kilmoylan, Co. Limerick.	U.
1768.*	,,	Grove, Co. Cork.	G.
1708.	,,	Jane, spinster, Dublin.	W.
1472.	,,	Joan.	T. & B., p.48.
1685.*	,,	John, Ballyellis, Co. Wexford.	M. v. XII, 156.
1688.	,,	John, Ballenbrake, Co. Cork.	G.
1718.*	,,	John, Cappagh, Co. Tipperary.	U.
1727.	,,	John, Mallow, Co. Cork	G.
1754.	,,	John, Kilburn, Co. Cork.	G.
1769.	,,	John Jervis, Ballyellis, Co. Wexford.	G.
1813.	,,	John, Ballinahinch.	W.
1740.	,,	Joseph, blacksmith, Cork.	G.
1727.	,,	Mark, Oxmantown, Co. Dublin.	W,
1821.	,,	Newport, late of Lisowen, now of Cashel.	U.
1727.	,,	Nicholas, Dublin.	W.
1476.	,,	Richard, Swords.	T. & B., p.33.
1766.*	,,	Susanna, spinster, Kilmoylan, Co. Limerick.	U.
1737.	,,	Swithin, Rochfordstown, Co. Cork.	G
1704.	,,	Symon, Knockcentry, Co. Limerick.	U.
1708.	,,	Walter, Pilcherstown, Co. Kildare.	W.
1683.	,,	William, Scurlogstown, Co. Westmeath.	W.
1744.	,,	William, dyer, Cork.	G.
1760.	,,	William, stay-maker, Cork.	G.

IRISH WILLS: COPIES AND ABSTRACTS.

Date of Probate.		REFERENCE
1774.	**White,** William, Cork.	G.
1813.	**Whitelaw,** Rev. James, Dublin.	W.
1729.	**Whiting,** Anne, Cork.	G.
1719.	,, John, alderman, Cork.	G.
1754.*	,, John, Mountrivers, Co. Cork.	G.
1800.	**Whitney,** Richard, Johnstown, Co. Cork.	G.
1665.	**Whitshed,** Esther, widow, Dublin.	W.
1728.	,, Mary, widow, Dublin.	W.
1664.	,, William, merchant, Dublin.	W.
1727.	,, William, Lord Chief Justice.	W.
1728.	**Whitsitt,** Joseph, Grange, Co. Tyrone.	W.
1682.	**Whittle,** Rev. John, Vicar of Dirrogh Diocese of Ossory.	W.
1473.	**Whyte,** Alice, Garristown.	T. & B., p.64.
1727.	**Wibault,** Major James.	W.
1667.	**Wickcomb,** Maud, alias **Cullen.**	W.
1719.	**Widenham,** Henry, Cork.	G.
1679.	,, John, Castletown, Co. Cork.	G.
1709.	,, John, Castletownroche, Co. Cork.	G.
1736.*	,, Mary, widow, Court, Co. Limerick.	G.
1725.	**Wight,** Thomas, clothier, Cork.	G.
1813.	**Wigmore,** William, Tipperary.	W.
1665.	**Wild,** George, Bishop of Derry.	W.
1729.	**Wilder,** Ellinor, widow, Castle Wilder, Co. Longford.	W
1813.	,, Stewart, an ensign in H.M. 18th Regiment of Foot.	W.
1728.	**Wilkinson,** Cuthbert, Sarsfield Court, Co. Cork.	G.
1729.	,, Elizabeth, widow, Magherdroll, Co. Down.	W.
1813.	,, Mary, Portarlington, Queen's Co.	W.
1708.	**Williams,** Edward, Dublin.	W.
1737.	,, Elizabeth, widow.	G.
1813.	,, Letitia, widow, Dublin.	W.
1710.	,, Margaret, alias **Loobey,** widow, Cork.	G.
1664.	,, Nathaniel, Dublin.	W.
1745.*	,, Oliver, Bealabahalla, Co. Cork.	G.
1640.	,, Owen, Newmarket, Co. Cork.	G.
1729.	,, Richard, Dublin.	W.

IRISH WILLS: COPIES AND ABSTRACTS.

Date of Probate.		REFERENCE.
1794.	**Williams,** Richardson, Dublin.	G.
1789.	,, Theodore, Ballyvonan, Co. Derry.	G.
1762.	,, Thomas, Rathcormack, Co. Cork.	G.
1804.	**Willington,** Charles, Eccles Street, Co. Dublin.	M. V. XII, 456
1813.	**Willison,** Ann, widow, Cork.	W.
1710.	**Wills,** Hannah, widow, Annagh, Co. Cork.	G.
1741.	,, Thomas, Cork.	G.
1655.	**Wilmer,** Captain Nathaniel, Cashel, Co. Tipperary.	G.
1726.	**Wilson,** Edward, merchant, Belfast.	W.
1813.	,, Hannah, Mount Prospect, Co. Kildare.	W.
1727.	,, John, Dublin.	W.
1728.	,, John, Killballybree, Co. Westmeath.	W.
1668.*	,, Sir Ralph, Kt., Cahirconlish, Co. Limerick.	S.
1671.	,, Rowland, Dublin.	W.
1813.	,, Walter, Maynooth.	W.
1729.	**Winckworth,** John, Maudlins, Co. Wexford.	W.
1728.	**Winnington,** Jane, widow, Dublin.	W.
1737.	**Wiseman,** John, Kilbonane, Co. Cork.	G.
1683.	,, Mary, alias **Venables,** widow, Wexford.	W. & G.
1665.	,, Ruth, widow, Dublin.	G.
1634.	,, William, Bandon, Co. Cork.	G.
1765.	,, William, Desure, Co. Cork.	G.
1813.	**Wolfe,** Bridget, Dunshaughlin, Co. Meath.	W.
1728.	**Wood,** Jane, alias **Croft,** widow, Dublin.	W.
1813.	,, Maria Letitia ,widow, Laurel Hill, Londonderry.	W.
1666.	**Woodfall,** Henry, tailor, Dublin.	W.
1798.	**Woodley,** Francis, Cork.	G.
1809.	,, Joseph, Cork.	G.
1665.	**Woodliffe,** Thomas, alderman, Cork.	G.
1658.*	**Woodrofe,** Ann, widow, Greenwich, Co. Kent.	W.
1662.	**Woodruffe,** Clement, Bandonbridge, Co. Cork.	G.
1784.	,, Samuel, Cork.	G.
1729.	**Woodside,** David, joiner, Dublin.	W.
1726.	**Woodward,** Charles, Drumbarrow, Co. Meath.	W.
1726.	**Workman,** Meredyth, Mahon, Co. Armagh.	W. & G

IRISH WILLS: COPIES AND ABSTRACTS.

Date of Probate.		REFERENCE
1727.	**Workman,** Thomas, Belfast.	W.
1810.*	**Worthervale,** Stephen, Co. Waterford.	G.
1666.	**Wray,** Henry, Castle Wray, Co. Donegal.	W.
1664.	**Wright,** Henry, Dublin.	W.
1757.*	,, John, merchant, Cork.	G.
1637.*	,, Richard, St. Finbarry, Cork.	G.
1714.	**Wrixon,** Henry, Ballygibbon, Co. Cork.	G.
1732.	,, Henry, Glinfield, Co. Cork.	G.
1778.	,, Henry, Blossomfort, Co. Cork.	G.
1787.*	,, Henry, Assolas, Co. Cork.	G.
1744.	,, John, Blossomfort, Co. Cork.	G.
1750.	,, Robert, Kilroe, Co. Cork.	G.
1768.*	,, Robert, Cork.	G.
1474.	**Wygth,** Nicholas, Lusk, Co. Dublin.	T. & B., p.111
1471.	**Wylde,** John, merchant.	T. & B., p.16
1726.	**Wyly,** John, farmer, Gilltown, Co. Kildare.	W.
1668.	**Wynne,** John, Killaltnagh, Co. Westmeath.	W.
1706.	**Wyse,** John, Ballynecourty, Co. Waterford.	W.
1813.	**Yeates,** Mary, widow, Armagh.	W
1699.	,, Robert, Dublin.	G
1744.*	**Yelverton,** William.	G.
1725.	**Yielding,** James, Tralee, Co. Kerry.	G.
1745.*	,, John, Tralee, Co. Kerry.	G.
1813.	**Young,** William, Nenagh, Co. Tipperary.	W.
1708.	**Ysarn,** John, Captain of Foot, late of Castres, France.	W.

N.B.—Re Report of the Deputy Keeper of the Records of Northern Ireland, mentioned in the Preface of this Volume, kindly note that the date there given is that of the year of publication, the Report itself being for the year 1927.

ERRATUM : Page 23. Reference Column. For " Y. Bandle " read " Y. Bundle."

LIST OF SUBSCRIBERS.

(Up to time of going to Press).

American Irish Historical Society, New York.
Barry, J. T., Ballyneety, Co. Limerick.
Bartley-Denniss, Lt.-Col. C., D.S.O., Lewes.
Bate, R. S., Bromley, Kent.
Belfast Central Public Library.
Benson, J. R., F.R.C.S., Alderholt. (2 copies).
Beresford, D. R. Pack, Bagnalstown, Ireland.
Blackwood, R. W., Belfast, Ireland.
Blake, Martin J., Maryborough, Ireland.
Bodleian Library, Oxford.
Boyce, C., M.D., Canford Cliffs, Dorset.
Bright, Mrs. M. Golding, London.
British Museum Library, London.
Burke, Sir H. Farnham, K.C.V.O., C.B., Garter
   King of Arms, College of Arms, London.
Butler, T. Blake, London.
Cain, R. C., Ballasalla Place, I.O.M.
Cambridge University Library.
Clements, H. J. B., London.
Coffey, Dr. B., Tralee, Co. Kerry.
Conner, Lt.-Col. D. G., O.B.E., Manch, Co. Cork.
Conner, H. L., B.L., Fort Robert, Co. Cork.
Cork University Library.
Corker, W., London.
Croby, Lt.-Col. W., D.S.O., Army and Navy Club,
   London.
Crozier, G., solicitor, Armagh, Ireland.
Cummins, Mrs. Ashley, Glanmere, Co. Cork.
Cunningham, Miss M. E., Waterloo, Larne, Ireland.
Cunningham, S., Fernhill, Belfast.
Cuthbert, General G. J., C.B., C.M.G., Hexham.
Darling, Rev. Canon H., Bective Rectory, Navan.
Dillon, J., Ballaghaderreen, Co. Mayo.
Dobbin, L., Cork.
Donegan, H. P. F., solicitor, Cork.
Drought, Maj. J. J., Kenya Colony.
Duggan and O'Reilly, solicitors, Dublin.
Dwelly, E., F.S.A.Scot., F.S.G., Fleet, Hants.
Elliott, William, Jr., New York.
Finnigan, C. J., Manchester.
Fletcher, L. L., F.R.S.A.I., Caterham Valley,
   Surrey.
Genealogists, Society of, London.
Gloucester Public Library.
Godfrey, Thomas, York. (2 copies).
Greeves, J. T., Knockdene Park, Knock, Belfast.
Griffin, H. F., Barnstable, Mass., U.S.A.
Guimaraens, A. J., London. (3 copies).
Hayden, Miss M., Rathmines, I.F.S.
Harrington, H. S., M.A., Dunloe Castle, Killarney.
   (4 copies).
Heuser, Dr. H. J., Overbrook, Philadelphia, U.S.A.
   (2 copies).
Hickie, Brig.-Gen. C. J., C.M.G., Borrisokane.
Hickie, M. D., D.L., Borrisokane, Co. Tipperary.
Hickie, Maj.-Gen. Sir W. B., K.C.B., Kildare-
   street Club, Dublin.
Hill, A., Bartley, Southampton.
Hodges, Figgis and Co., booksellers, Dublin. (6
   copies).
John Rylands Library, Manchester.
Johnston, T. G., Cultra, Holywood, Belfast.
Kirkpatrick, T. P. C., M.D., Dublin.
Lee, P. G., M.D., F.R.S.A.I., Cork.
Lepper, R. S., Ulster Club, Belfast. (2 copies).
Lett, Miss A. L. K., Kilculler, Co. Kildare.

Leviss, H. F., D.Litt., Bournemouth.
Liverpool Reference Library.
Long, F. C., St. Luke's, Cork.
Longford, Dr. W. U. D., Holywood, Belfast.
Lowry-Corry, The Lady Dorothy, Castle Coole,
   Enniskillen, Ireland.
McCarthy, G. F., Dublin.
McGuirk, Rev. J., P.P., Rush, Co. Dublin.
MacInerny, Rev. M. H., O.P., Dublin.
Macnamara, D. W., Bankyle, Corofin, Co. Clare.
Madan, F., Brasenose College, Oxford.
Maine Historical Society, Portland, U.S.A.
Manchester Reference Library.
Martin, H.R., Richmond Herald, College of Arms.
Maunsell, H. R., Dublin.
Max, J. T., Llanfairfechan, N. Wales.
Minns, G., Salt Lake City, Utah, U.S.A.
Mitchell, J. D., Parsonstown, King's Co.
Nash, Lt.-Col. E., J.P., Broomfield, Essex.
Nash, Sir Vincent, Kt., Limerick.
National Library of Ireland, Dublin.
National Library of Scotland, Edinburgh.
Needham, T. A., B.A., Chapel-en-le-Frith.
New York Historical Society.
New York Public Library.
O'Donoghue, T., University College, Cork.
Office of Arms, Dublin Castle.
O'Hegarty, P. S., Rathgar, Dublin.
O'Leary, P., Graignamanagh, Co. Kilkenny.
O'Loughlin, C., Dublin. (2 copies).
Pennsylvania Historical Society, Philadelphia,
   U.S.A.
Phelps, E., Monkstown, Co. Dublin.
Plunkett, G. N., Count, K.C.H.S., Dublin.
Poë, Lt.-Col. Sir Hutcheson, Bart., C.B., Batch-
   wood Hall, Herts.
Potter, Lt.-Col. W. A., D.S.O., Woodborough,
   Notts.
Public Record Office, Belfast.
Read, A. W., Leicester.
Relton, A., Hove, Sussex.
Rice, Rev. J. Ballindangan, Co. Cork.
Rogerson, T. Cooper, Hove, Sussex.
Royal Dublin Society Library.
Rudkin, Major H. R., Compton, Guildford.
Russell, J., Bath.
Scully, J., Blackrock, Co., Dublin.
Stafford, Rev. R. G., London.
Stationery Office, Dublin. (2 copies).
Steele, Rev. W. B., Levally, Enniskillen, Co. Fer-
   managh.
Stephenson, Miss J., Washington, U.S.A.
Swanzy, Rev. Canon, M.R.I.A., Newry, Co., Down.
Tibbs, Rev. P. G., M.A., Hargrave, Huntingdon.
Tipperary County Library, Thurles, Ireland.
Toppin, A., F.S.A., Bluemantle, College of Arms,
   London.
Trinity College Library, Dublin.
Trinity College Library, Hartford, Conn., U.S.A.
Upton, H. A., M.R.I.A., Coolatore, Co. Westmeath.
Walford Bros., London (2 copies).
Waters, E. W., Brideweir, Conna, Co. Cork.
Welply, C. H., Ulster Club, Belfast.
White, Col. J. Grove, C.M.G., Kilbyrne, Co. Cork.
Wilson, L., Barrow-in-Furness.
Woollaston, J. Woods, College of Arms, London.